CONTENTS

A SHORT
INTRODUCTION

That which does not kill me, makes me stronger.[1]

(Friedrich Nietzsche)

Courage seems to me the whole pre-history of man.[2]

(Friedrich Nietzsche)

Throughout our long history, humankind has been remarkably successful at overcoming adversity and thriving on the opportunities presented by the world in which we live. You could argue that humans are one of the hardiest species to inhabit the earth. Theories of evolution claim that abilities and attributes that aid in survival are passed on from generation to generation, because the individual passing them on lived long enough to have children. Given the length of time humans have been evolving in their present form (roughly 30,000 years), it might be argued that all people have within them the inherited potential to be resilient.

Ensuring that children achieve their potential to be resilient is a universal concern of parents, caregivers and professionals who work with children. A child's capacity to cope with adversity and 'stand on their own two feet' is seen by those who have a caring concern for children as an important part of development, and essential in order to achieve independence and success in later life. Perhaps just as universal is the concern for shielding children from physical and emotional distress. These seemingly competing concerns are a source of confusion and heartache for those who have the best interests of children at heart, and have the potential to obscure an understanding of what is, indeed, in a child's best interests. I wrote this book in order to provide parents, caregivers and professionals who work with children a clear vision of how to ensure that children realize their natural inheritance to be resilient, without precipitating conflicts and confusion about a child's best interests.

Resilience as a specific characteristic or attribute of a person can be difficult to pin down. A review of the professional literature uncovers a long list of characteristics that are observed in resilient people, and hence are thought to be characteristics of resilience. For the purpose of achieving clarity about what resilience is and how it can be nurtured, I have confined myself to three key aspects of resilience in this book, incorporating biological, psychological and environmental aspects. These aspects are *arousal*, *attachment* and *needs-provision* (more on this terminology later). I will look at the implications of these aspects on resilience in children, and present the reader with practical advice and strategies for increasing resilience in children in relation to each of the three aspects.

Throughout the book I have opted to use one gender, 'he' or 'she', when giving examples of the concepts I am presenting. I have done this for ease of reading rather than to suggest a condition is more common in boys or girls.

The glossary at the end of this book is included to inform and clarify my own interpretation of various terms, and is a reflection of my general concern for making the subject matter accessible to those who may not be familiar with specialist terminology and jargon. As such, it is not intended to be a glossary of professional terms; nor is it intended for professional use only. Rather, I anticipate that the glossary will help readers attain a full and satisfying understanding of my experiences and perspectives concerning resilience. Finally, I tend to use the generic term 'caregiver', as opposed to the more specific term 'parent'. I have done so in order to reinforce my contention that the information and strategies contained in this book are relevant to all adults who are involved with children in a caregiving role and in making decisions about children.

Colby Pearce
January 2011

PROLOGUE

A TALE OF FOUR CHILDREN AND THEIR TRIP TO THE ADVENTURE PLAYGROUND

Once upon a time there were four children. On a warm and sunny day the parents of each child took them to an adventure playground.

The first child had a wonderful time. He confidently swung on the swings, slid on the slippery-slides, toured the tunnels, and flew on the flying fox. Under the watchful gaze of his parents he tried everything and excitedly reported his feats of bravery and accomplishment to them. His parents accompanied him to each item of equipment and warmly acknowledged his efforts. They even tried some of the more difficult items to demonstrate what was possible and remained close by to catch their child if he should fall. Upon leaving the playground this child sought acknowledgement from his parents that he could come again another day.

The second child bounded from his parents' car and eagerly entered the adventure playground, not noticing that his parents remained in the car. Observing many children at the giant slippery-slide he excitedly approached it for a go. He was unconcerned that the other children at the slippery-slide were much older than him and that it was very high and very fast. He did not notice, nor did anyone tell him, that the slide was better suited for older children. He flew off the bottom and cannoned into the ground, hurting his arm. Shock and pain turned to tearful distress as he could not immediately find his parents to console him. By the time his parents arrived, he was difficult to soothe and angrily refused to try any other equipment. His anger and distress quickly escalated and he was carried, screaming, from the playground.

The third child approached the playground much more cautiously, preferring to remain close to his parents, holding hands. His parents guided him to the quietest corner of the playground, where the smallest and safest equipment could be found. They held his hand or carried him in their lap on the swings and the slide. When he gazed wistfully at the other children his age who were re-enacting tales of bravery and heroism in a fort, his parents encouraged him to remain with them in the sand-pit. His parents delighted in his company, and he in theirs, and he readily agreed that the fort looked dangerous and the other children played too rough.

The fourth child never made it to the adventure playground as his parents could not afford to buy fuel for their car. He spent the day alternately demanding to be taken to the playground and sulking about not being able to go.

CHAPTER **1**

UNDERSTANDING RESILIENCE

He who has a why to live for can bear with almost any how.[3]
(Friedrich Nietzsche)

Reflecting on this famous quote from the nineteenth-century German philosopher Friedrich Nietzsche, psychiatrist Viktor Frankl prepared one of the most famous books on twentieth-century psychology and psychiatry.

Held prisoner in Nazi concentration camps during the Second World War, Dr Frankl made a detailed study of his fellow inmates, and aspects of the psychological functioning of those who survived longest and those who quickly succumbed to their predicament. He observed that those who could find meaning in (that is, a purpose or reason for) their suffering survived best in the face of adversity. The meaning he made of his own suffering was that, though he found himself in terrible circumstances, he was learning some very valuable lessons about human survival in conditions of adversity. Having found a reason for his suffering he was able to survive in order to share his insights with the world. These insights, and his experiences in concentration camps, formed the subject matter of his famous work *Man's Search for Meaning.*[4]

Nietzsche considered that we learn and grow through our exposure to adversity. Frankl believed that the meaning we make of our suffering determines whether we survive it or not. This is poignantly illustrated in his story about the aging doctor who consulted him for depression after his wife had passed away two years earlier.[5] As Frankl tells it, the doctor was not coping and was in deep distress. Frankl asked the doctor what he thought his wife would have been like if she had been the one to survive him. The doctor apparently responded that she would have been similarly distressed. Upon hearing this, Frankl advised the doctor that in surviving his wife he had spared her great suffering. Frankl reported that the doctor said nothing, calmly shook his hand and left the room. Frankl concluded that suffering ends when it finds a meaning, such as the meaning of a sacrifice.[6]

Many of us, when reflecting on the challenging times we have faced in our lives, can identify how we have benefited as a result of our trials and tribulations and success in moving beyond them. Although Frankl's treatise is a worthy one, it is probably not the case that individuals of all ages, particularly children, pause to consider what meaning they might make of their suffering in the face of adversity. And yet, by one means or another, children and adults do cope with adversity, and benefit from doing so. So what characteristics and abilities do we have that assist us to cope with adversity and gain experiences of achievement and self-esteem from having done so? This is the subject matter of this book, with the particular focus being on what assists children to cope with adversity.

Adversity features in the life of every child. It can be present when a child is learning a new skill, on their first day of school, when they are negotiating conflicts and when ambition exceeds ability. For some children, such as those who have chronic medical conditions and disabilities, adversity is a predominant and pervasive feature of their day-to-day life. Some children demonstrate persistence in the face of adverse conditions, whereas others shy away from them. Whatever the source of adversity, the ability to cope with it is critical to a child's development and to them experiencing a productive, successful and satisfying life.

My own childhood was marked by chronic teasing and harassment at school. The teasing and harassment began when I was approximately seven years of age and persisted throughout my primary and secondary schooling. It carried over to the sporting club at which I was a member, where many children from my school were also members. It was constant. Similarly, as an adult, I experienced bullying and harassment in the workplace. Nevertheless, though I did not enjoy school or my workplace, I attended every day, missing neither school nor work for reasons of avoiding having to face up to these adverse conditions.

So what enabled me to consistently confront situations of adversity? Well, as a child I engaged in prodigious amounts of physical activity, which was an important source of feelings of achievement and self-esteem (that is, mastery) and a stress release. Throughout my childhood, teenage years and young adulthood I was heavily involved in church youth groups, where I had the friendship, respect and admiration of peers and adults alike and was a leader among my peers. Also, I enjoyed strong emotional connections within an extended family network. I coped well with schoolwork and work demands, such that both environments were places of mastery, as well as misery. My experiences of mastery were crucial in nurturing my capacity to confront difficult circumstances, and overcome them.

Psychological strength, or *resilience*, is directly implicated in a child's capacity to cope with adversity. Resilience represents that quality of the individual that enables them to persist in the face of challenges and recover from difficulty or hardship. Resilience strengthens a child and enables them to try new experiences, accept challenges, and cope with frustration and failure. Resilience sustains a child through hardship and supports the realization of personal dreams and aspirations. As such, the promotion of resilience is a universal concern of all adults with a caring concern for children.

In my own experience, notwithstanding my traumatic experiences at school, I persisted with my education and ended up realizing my ambition of attending university. Though I did not know it at the time, less than one per cent of individuals who commenced first year psychology when I did, went on to complete a Masters Degree in Clinical Psychology and practice as a clinical psychologist.

I achieved this goal in eight years instead of the usual six. Though I took a little longer, I achieved my goal. I did so notwithstanding the potentially debilitating effects of temporal lobe epilepsy, diagnosed when I was 17 years old and in my first year of university, and the medication used to control this condition. I vividly recall the neurologist who diagnosed my condition advising me that I should withdraw from my studies, get at least eight hours sleep every night, and abstain from drinking too much alcohol. In particular, I remember him advising me that, in view of my condition, I would be most suited to working at the level of a production worker in a factory environment. Upon arriving home from the consultation I broke down. This was the first and last time I cried about my condition. Afterwards, I persisted in working towards my academic goals, preferring to ignore the advice of my neurologist.

Later, when my application for entrance into various Masters Degrees in Clinical Psychology at universities across Australia was rejected, I was unemployed for approximately eight months. During this time I applied for dozens of jobs as a research assistant and was not offered even a single interview. Eventually, a friend who did her Honours year with me suggested me to her employers, as she was leaving to travel overseas. Her employer was the local child and adolescent mental health service and I remained there as a research officer for approximately five years, publishing seven research papers on adolescent mental health in international psychiatric journals. I left this employment to work as a clinical psychologist in child protection, achieving a standing in the community that supported my transition into private practice approximately seven years later. I have taught child clinical psychology to Masters and Doctoral students in Clinical Psychology and have been the Director of University training clinics. I have supervised the development of 50 practising psychologists. I daresay that had I been less resilient none of this would have been possible.

Children cope with adversity in different ways. For example, many children experience anxiety about taking tests. Some children study up on the subject matter of the test beforehand in order to feel more confident about their knowledge. In doing so, they gradually expose themselves to feelings of anxiety, but not necessarily to the point of being overwhelmed. On the day of the test they are less likely to be anxious because they are better prepared and have had a number of experiences of coping with anxiety. Other children try to not think about taking the test altogether, and don't practise. These children also reduce their anxiety, until the day of the test that is. Not only are they more likely to experience uncomfortable levels of anxiety on that day, they are less likely to perform as well as the child who prepared themself.

Some coping strategies improve the child's circumstances under conditions of adversity, and hence are adaptive. Adaptive coping strategies include problem-solving, breaking a task down into its smaller component parts and mastering each component of the task, accessing the support of others and persisting in one's efforts.

Other coping strategies provide temporary relief from conditions of adversity, but ultimately do not improve the child's circumstances. These latter coping strategies are maladaptive. Maladaptive coping strategies include giving up, avoidance, drug-taking and affective displays (for example tantrums). I believe that resilience incorporates the application of adaptive coping skills under conditions of adversity, such that a child's circumstances and future capacity to cope with adversity are maintained or enhanced.

A child's capacity to cope with adversity (that is, their resilience) varies over time in association with biological, psychological and environmental influences, and the interaction of these.

Biological influences include the child's temperament and their susceptibility to stress and anxiety. Psychological influences include the child's capacity to develop and maintain constructive beliefs in conditions of adversity, including beliefs about personal worth and competence, expectations of social support and beliefs about the world in which they live. Environmental influences include the extent to which the environment satisfies the needs of the child, including the child's need for love, acceptance, protection, safety, shelter and physical sustenance. Physiological, psychological and environmental influences affect the extent to which a child can get on with exploring their world, achieve their potential and lead a successful and satisfying life, without the debilitating and restricting effects of anxiety and its common symptom, avoidance.

BIOLOGICAL INFLUENCES

Exposure to adversity is critical to the development and maintenance of adaptive skills and attributes for managing life's challenges, and for the realization of dreams and aspirations.

However, exposure to adversity must be balanced with the need to care for and protect children from the debilitating effects of prolonged emotional distress. Emotional distress is associated with high levels of activity in the body's nervous systems, including the brain and extended nerve systems that regulate muscle control and movement. We refer to the level of activation of the body's nervous systems as *arousal*.

High levels of arousal occur when the individual is under pressure or experiencing anxiety. High levels of arousal are known to impact adversely on performance, learning and the likelihood a child will attempt a new task and succeed. This is readily exemplified by a child attempting to walk the length of a balance-beam. If the balance-beam is raised to the height of two feet, most school-aged children would be confident that they could walk the entire length, would readily give it a go, and would experience a sense of achievement and mastery upon their likely successful completion of this task.

However, if the balance-beam was raised to a height of eight feet, most school-aged children would be concerned about falling and hurting themselves. Though they might already have successfully walked its length at a lower height, they would doubt their ability to accomplish the task without injury, with the result that they would experience fear and distress and their arousal would be elevated. Elevated physiological arousal brings with it a range of physical sensations, including butterflies in the stomach, dizziness, tingling, tremors and shortness of breath, each of which serve as a distraction and impediment to smooth and coordinated movement. In combination with emotional distress, most children are likely to find these sensations unpleasant and distracting.

In an attempt to relieve their emotional distress and associated unpleasant and distracting physiological sensations, many children would simply avoid trying this more difficult task, with the result that their fear and distress would subside. Others, who do try, might find that their balance and movements are impaired by their feelings of dizziness and tremulousness. Though they may successfully complete the task, they may well have found it so distressing that they are unwilling to attempt it a second time.

However, if the child is reassured that they will not be injured if they fall from the higher balance-beam, because gym mats have been placed underneath, the child is likely to be less fearful and willing to attempt a more difficult task and succeed. Similarly, as physiological arousal varies with emotional intensity, the child who experiences lower levels of physiological arousal under conditions of adversity is likely to be less susceptible to physical and emotional distress, and more likely to accept challenges and experience thoughts of personal competence and mastery. Hence, the capacity to maintain lower levels of physiological arousal under conditions of adversity is an important component of resilience.

In Chapter 2 I will discuss the issue of arousal in more detail and present strategies for maintaining optimum levels of arousal.

PSYCHOLOGICAL INFLUENCES

Caregiving plays a critical role in promoting resilience in children. Caregiving that promotes resilience strikes a balance between encouraging acceptance of risks and protection from harm, such as occurs when a parent stands at the base of the ladder while their child negotiates a slippery-slide, or holds their child's hand while they cross a busy road. Caregivers who support and encourage their children to accept risks and challenges, at the same time protecting them from the debilitating and disempowering effects of prolonged emotional distress and repeated or overwhelming failure, ensure experiences of 'mastery'. Mastery experiences are critical in the development of a perception of personal competence and capacity to influence personal outcomes.

A child's preparedness to explore their internal (thoughts, feelings, sensations) and external worlds is an essential ingredient in them achieving their developmental potential and having full and satisfying life experiences. This exploration is profoundly influenced by the special relationship a child develops with their main caregiver(s) during the first four years of their life. Referred to as the child's *attachment* to their primary caregivers, this aspect of the psychological make-up of the child also plays a key role in the development of the child's beliefs about personal worth and competence, their expectations of social support, and their perceptions of the world in which they live.

Consider three one-year-old infants. One is developing a *secure* attachment to her caregivers. The other two infants are *insecure*. As a result of her having experienced her caregivers as accessible to her, sensitive to her needs and responsive to those needs, the secure infant will confidently move away from her caregiver in order to explore her physical and social world. From time to time she will return to her caregiver before moving away again. Increasingly, she will merely orient visually to her caregiver and vocalize to her. All the while she is exploring and experiencing her physical, emotional and social world. Her motor and cognitive development is stimulated through her play. Her social and language development are stimulated through her interactions with others. Her emotional development is stimulated through shared and varied emotional experiences. Her future capacity to achieve milestones like bladder and bowel control is enhanced by her preparedness to pay attention to sensations in her body. And all the time she is developing knowledge and skills that make her better able to cope with her world.

In contrast, the insecure infants are either clingy and obsessed with the parent, or appear disengaged from the parent and others. One seeks to be held all the time and protests being placed on the floor. She is fearful and requires constant reassurance. Her preoccupation with safety and the accessibility and responsiveness of her caregiver, arising from inconsistent care, limits her experiences, her exploration and her play, and hence, all aspects of her development. The other infant has apparently learnt that adults are consistently undependable and that interacting with them is a pointless, distressing, and even a frightening activity. Though appearing uninterested, she is likely to be highly fearful as she perceives that she must take care of herself in a world that is uncaring and potentially unsafe. Her fearfulness reduces the likelihood of exploration, thereby also impacting adversely on all aspects of her development and her emotional well-being, including her ability to cope with her world.

In Chapter 3 I will describe attachment in more detail and approaches to care and management that facilitate attachment security.

ENVIRONMENTAL INFLUENCES

In order for children to achieve their developmental potential and lead a full and satisfying life, they need to believe that they are able to satisfy needs that are essential to their survival and happiness. The love, care, acceptance and protection of an adult caregiver who is thought of as better able to cope with the world are examples of needs that, when consistently met, ensure that children survive and thrive. Shelter and physical sustenance are also important needs that must be met. In the absence of a reliable satisfaction of needs that are essential to their survival and happiness, children become anxious. Their anxiety activates the parts of the brain that control instinctive survival responses and de-activates those parts of the brain that are responsible for logical thinking, planning, and effective action.[7] They become demanding and difficult to reason with. They are typically resistant to having their attention diverted elsewhere. Continued denial of their attempts to secure a response to their needs often results in an escalation of their anxiety. Gaining satisfaction of their needs becomes the most important objective in the child's life in that moment – an apparent matter of survival, with the result that they display a restricted range of interest and behaviour until such time that their needs are consistently met.

This restricted range of interest and behaviour limits the child's capacity to live life to the full and perform daily tasks. This is most obvious among maltreated children who, having been denied consistent access to sensitive and loving care, exhibit a limited range of interests and a propensity to engage in controlling and coercive patterns of relating to others. They do so in particular towards adults in a caregiving role, in order to reassure themselves that they have access to their needs.

In my own experience, I have observed my children become anxious, unreasonably demanding and resistant to redirection when the demands of running a family business have caused my wife and me to be preoccupied and less accessible to them. Though their demands may involve something as simple as having one of us play a game with them or to have us fix them a snack, their real need is for our time and attention.

It is important to remember that needs are often expressed as simple requests and wishes. It is also important to consider that in the denial of simple requests and wishes we may be denying the child fulfilment of a vital need. This is where responding to our children with understanding is so important. Consistently demonstrating understanding of our children's real needs and responding to them is reassuring to the child, with the result that they can get on with exploring all that their world offers without experiencing the debilitating and restricting effects of anxiety.

The role of accessibility to needs-provision and strategies to enhance it will be presented in more detail in Chapter 4.

CHAPTER SUMMARY

- Adversity features in the life of every child.

- The ability to cope with adversity is critical to a child's development and to them experiencing a productive, successful and satisfying life.

- Psychological strength, or *resilience*, is directly implicated in a child's capacity to cope with adversity.

- Resilience represents that quality of the individual that enables them to persist in the face of challenges and recover from difficulty or hardship.

- Resilience strengthens a child and equips them to try new experiences, accept challenges, and cope with frustration and failure.

- Resilience sustains a child through hardship and supports the realization of personal dreams and aspirations.

- Resilience incorporates the application of adaptive coping skills under conditions of adversity, such that a child's circumstances and future capacity to deal with adversity are maintained or enhanced.

- Adaptive coping strategies improve the child's circumstances under conditions of adversity. These strategies include problem-solving, breaking a task down into its smaller component parts and mastering each component of the task, accessing the support of others and persisting in one's efforts.

- Maladaptive coping strategies provide temporary relief from conditions of adversity, but do not improve the child's circumstances. Maladaptive strategies for coping include giving up, avoidance, drug-taking and affective displays (e.g. tantrums).

- Exposure to adversity is critical to the development and maintenance of adaptive skills and attributes for managing challenges associated with daily living, and for the realization of dreams and aspirations. However, exposure to adversity must be balanced with the need to care for and protect children from the debilitating effects of prolonged emotional distress.

- Resilience varies over time in association with biological, psychological and environmental influences, and the interaction of these.

- Biological influences are manifested in the child's capacity to reason and solve problems (i.e. a child's intellectual potential), in their temperament, and in their susceptibility to stress and anxiety.

- Psychological influences include the child's capacity to develop and maintain constructive beliefs in conditions of adversity, including beliefs about personal worth and competence, expectations of social support and beliefs about the world in which they live.

- Environmental influences include the extent to which the environment satisfies the needs of the child, including the child's need for love, acceptance, protection, safety, shelter and physical sustenance.

- Parenting plays a critical role in promoting resilience in children. Caregiving that promotes resilience strikes a balance between encouraging acceptance of risks and protection from harm.

CHAPTER 2

BIOLOGICAL INFLUENCES – AROUSAL

He who is master of himself is the Superman.[8]

Have you ever had the experience where you have been attempting to solve a problem, you have become frustrated and annoyed with your apparent inability to do so, you take a short break, and when you come back to the problem the answer seems simple and you readily achieve a solution? Have challenging tasks ever seemed insurmountable when faced but manageable, on reflection, when successfully completed?

Undoubtedly, the answer is 'yes' to both. So, how is this possible? What is going on here? The answer lies in our understanding of *arousal* and how it impacts on performance of daily tasks.

In simple terms, arousal refers to the level of activity of the body's nervous systems. Arousal goes up and down during the day, depending on a person's mood, what they are doing and what is happening in their environment, much like in Figure 2.1.

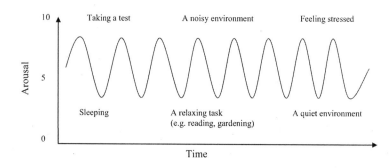

Figure 2.1 Arousal across time

Arousal is generally lowest when we are asleep and highest when we are in a state of high emotion. Arousal is regulated by the brain. In ordinary circumstances, arousal is thought to go up and down within a regular range, which varies from person to person. Each person's range of arousal varies as a result of genetic inheritance, early exposure to stress, ongoing maintaining factors, and the interaction of these. The temperament infants are born with is involved, as 'easy babies' seemingly maintain lower levels of arousal, whereas 'slow-to-warm-up' and 'difficult' babies maintain higher levels of arousal.

Early stressors include pregnancy and birth complications, early illness, neglect and maltreatment. Early stressors are thought to impact on the structure of the developing brain, particularly those structures that are responsible for the control, or regulation, of arousal.[9] Frequent exposure to stress and prolonged distress, particularly during the first year of life, is thought to result in significant development of the parts of the brain that are associated with high arousal and emotional distress. The result of this is that the central nervous system (i.e. the brain) becomes hard-wired to be highly reactive to sensory stimulation (i.e. sights, sounds, touch, taste, smell) and perceived threats, and vulnerable to maintaining higher levels of arousal. Maintaining factors include stressors that increase arousal, including bullying and harassment, learning difficulties and traumatic family circumstances. These also include strength factors that support lower arousal, such as the presence of loving and supportive relationships.

A conventional term for people whose arousal fluctuates in the higher range is that these people are 'highly-strung'. Conversely, a conventional term for people whose arousal fluctuates in the lower range is that these people are 'laid-back'. *Highly-strung* individuals are on-the-go, intense, and make mountains out of molehills. *Laid-back* individuals are observed to be relaxed, calm, unflappable and resilient. As is represented in Figure 2.2, it seems to take a lot more stimulation and adversity for laid-back individuals to experience stress (C). In contrast, highly-strung individuals are more prone to stress (A), and its associated negative consequences, than laid-back individuals.

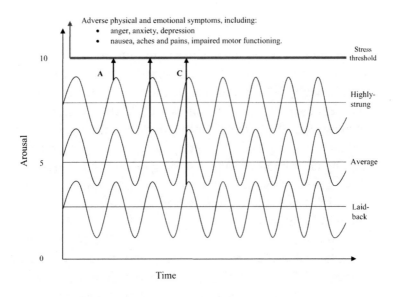

Figure 2.2 The relationship between arousal and vulnerability to stress

So what is the relationship between arousal and performance of daily activities? Well, the answer is represented in Figure 2.3, which shows that we need to be aroused to a certain level in order to perform at our best.

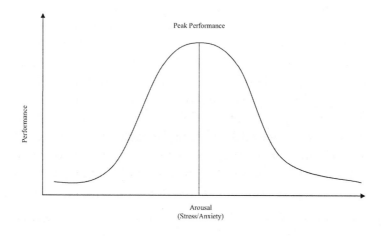

Figure 2.3 The relationship between arousal and performance

When arousal is too low, or too high, our best performance is not possible. This can be illustrated by research into the 'Mozart Effect'.[10] Proponents of the Mozart Effect claimed that exposure to certain forms of classical music could increase your IQ. Support for the Mozart Effect was based on research that showed that performance on certain problem-solving tasks improved after listening to music by Mozart.[11, 12] Such research became popularized[13] and assertions were made that listening to relaxing classical music could improve the IQ of children.[14]

Unfortunately, further research into this phenomenon complicated the issue. Some researchers found no Mozart Effect.[15] Other researchers found that it disappeared when the contribution of changes in mood and arousal associated with listening to the music were removed.[16] This led to the conclusion that temporary improvement in performance on certain problem-solving tasks has more to do with the relative effects of music on arousal, with some types of music producing a state of arousal conducive to improved or optimal performance.[17]

I think of arousal as being a gauge of resilience, much like a thermometer is a gauge of body temperature. With body temperature, there is an optimum range, around 37 degrees celsius, at which all of us, children included, are physically well. When body temperature gets too high, it is a sign that a child is not well. When temperature is too low, it is a sign that a child has hypothermia. When arousal is too high, a child's performance deteriorates and they experience physical and emotional distress. Mastery experiences are less likely and the child is vulnerable to repeated failure in their efforts to complete daily tasks. The result is that their self-confidence is undermined and their ability to cope with adversity is reduced. In contrast, if we can maintain a child's arousal in the middle part of the range they are more likely to perform at their best, to have mastery experiences and to feel capable and competent when faced with adversity. So, in order to promote resilience in children we need to understand the relationship between arousal and performance, and to implement strategies to maintain optimum levels of arousal.

So, what about people who claim to work better under pressure? How is this possible? Well, we all need a certain amount of stimulation or pressure in order to perform at our peak. Our discussion of laid-back and highly-strung individuals suggests that some people cope better with, and may in fact require, a certain amount of pressure in order to perform at their peak. Others, being already highly aroused, require little additional stimulation or pressure to perform at their peak, and may actually need to take action to reduce their arousal in order to perform at their peak. It all depends on the range in which our arousal typically varies. Nevertheless, even the most laid-back person can be placed under enough pressure that their performance is impaired, as is exemplified in high-pressure television quiz shows such as *Minute to Win It*. In *Minute to Win It* contestants complete a series of tasks in order to win increasing amounts of prize money, much like what occurs in other game shows such as *Who Wants to be a Millionaire*. Contestants have three 'lives', which they can use when they fail to complete a set task. Tasks at which the contestant fails must be repeated until the contestant is successful, or until they run out of lives. When a contestant fails at a task they often do worse and worse on successive attempts. As the pressure to succeed increases, their performance deteriorates.

High levels of arousal are associated with anxiety problems in children. The most salient symptom of anxiety is avoidance of the source of anxiety. Anxious children might seek to control aspects of their life, including others, in order to avoid the source of their anxiety. They might avoid situations in which they have to confront the object of their fear, or they might avoid thinking about the source of their anxiety. They might engage in a combination of these. Whatever their pattern of responding to the source of their fear and worry, anxiety has a negative impact on the child's ability to cope with adverse circumstances. It follows that anxiety has a negative impact on a child's resilience.

Anxious children are prone to behaviours associated with the fight/flight/freeze response. This phenomenon, which includes controlling, aggressive and destructive behaviours (fight), running, hiding and hyperactivity (flight), and decreased responsiveness to the environment or 'shutting down' (freeze), is considered to be an automatic response to anxiety. The fight/flight/freeze response is the body's way of dealing with the negative physical and emotional symptoms of anxiety. Its function is to lower arousal and produce feelings of physical and emotional well-being by neutralizing a perceived threat or removing the person from the proximity of a perceived threat.

The fight/flight/freeze response to heightened arousal/ anxiety is considered to have been 'naturally selected' through evolution. Its role is to facilitate a return to feelings of safety and well-being in the face of threats to the individual. By 'natural selection' we mean the idea that characteristics of a species that aid in survival tend to be passed on genetically from generation to generation because they keep the individual alive long enough to reproduce. The fight/flight/freeze response is activated by the parts of the brain that are responsible for instinctive reactions and those that are necessary for survival.[18] Many of these responses, such as emotion, body temperature, breathing and arousal, are not consciously experienced all the time. This means that when children exhibit behaviours as a result of the fight/ flight/freeze response, they may well do so instinctively and without apparent consideration of what they are doing and what will be the consequences of their actions.

My home is in a bush habitat and a winter creek flows through the property. In one section of the creek-bed the banks are retained with old wooden railway sleepers. A brown snake is regularly spotted moving through my property by neighbours who look down into my yard. The snake appears to follow a well-worn path that ends very close to the old railway sleepers. The nooks and crannies between the sleepers must make a good habitat for a brown snake.

Approximately three years ago, in mid-autumn, my wife and I cut back plants that had invaded the creek in the vicinity of the sleepers. It was a warm sunny day. I expected to encounter a snake, but did not in all the time I was cutting and clearing away. However, later in the day, as I was standing still and spraying poison on the remnant stalks of the plants, I gazed to the left and immediately saw a five-foot brown snake slithering straight towards me, approximately three metres away. I immediately felt chilled and the hairs stood up on my neck. I froze. I then jumped out of the creek. As I did so I bent and picked up a rock, turned and threw at the snake in one motion. Freeze–flight–fight. At each step I did not have time to consider my position and actions, nor was I conscious of having done so. I acted instinctively.

However, afterwards I was aware that I had, in fact made an assessment of the distance between me and the snake and my chances of getting away. I was also aware that I had noticed that the snake was extended to its full length and less likely to be able to leap at me. I am unsure if these were rationalizations after the fact. I am sure that I was not thinking such thoughts in the midst of my fight/flight/freeze experience.

Unfortunately, the behavioural manifestations of the fight/flight/freeze response are rarely perceived by adults in a caregiving role as the body's normal mechanism for coping with anxiety, nor are they perceived as being instinctive and unconscious. Rather, adults in a caregiving role typically and erroneously assert that the child knows what they are doing and can control their emotions and associated actions. As a result, these behaviours are often responded to with anger and discipline, with the result that the anxious child's hyper-aroused state is likely to be maintained, or even made worse. And yet, on the basis of what we now know about how the brain works when a person is stressed, it may not always be possible for children to simply control their intense emotions, high arousal and associated fight/flight/freeze behaviours.[19]

Brain imaging studies show that when an individual is under stress, or when an individual is exposed to sensory stimulation associated with past traumatic events, there is significant activation of sub-cortical (inner) regions of the brain and reduced blood flow to areas of the frontal cortex[20, 21] (outer, frontal regions of the brain). The areas of frontal cortex of the brain that experience reduced blood flow are thought to be those that are responsible for logical, rational thinking, planning and responding, and speech. The sub-cortical regions of the brain are responsible for instinctive responses and those that are essential to the survival of the organism, such as emotion, respiration, arousal and the fight/flight/ freeze response. It follows that when a child is in distress their capacity to think and reason logically, and express themself verbally in order to control their emotions, is reduced. Experience shows that if a child is distressed enough, their capacity to think and reason logically is almost non-existent. At such times, children require the intervention of adults in a caregiving role to articulate the child's experience and assist them in the modulation of their arousal levels and associated emotions.

Arousal impacts on a child's capacity to perform at his or her best and experience mastery. Mastery experiences are critical to the development of beliefs about self-worth and potency that are beneficial to the individual. Those who persist in their efforts under adverse conditions and succeed develop a more positive perception of their competency and future ability to manage adversity. Arousal is also implicated in emotional functioning, with high arousal levels associated with adjustment problems and anxiety in children. Hence, arousal, and its regulation, is an important component of endeavours to promote resilience in children.

MANAGING AROUSAL

So, given that arousal is such a crucial factor influencing resilience in children, how do we manage it so that:

1. children have a greater tolerance for adverse circumstances

2. they are more likely to perform at their best and experience mastery, and

3. their self-confidence and belief in their ability to cope with adversity is nurtured?

In my professional experience, the most simple and effective method for reducing arousal and achieving greater tolerance for adversity during the day is to play soothing classical music quietly in the child's bedroom all night, every night.[22]

Consider the fact that when we are asleep we still awaken to noises in our sleeping environment. This means that while we are unconscious our brain is still paying attention to what is going on around us. So why not take advantage of this and deliberately expose the brain to noise that is relaxing and soothing? Referring to the earlier discussion of the Mozart Effect, music can be used to produce states of arousal that help us to perform at our best.

As arousal is a significant element of emotion, playing soothing classical music throughout the night can be used to produce feelings of emotional well-being as well as physiological relaxation, with the result that children in your care will sleep more soundly, wake happier and be more tolerant of stimulation in the day ahead. They will start the day with a lower state of arousal, and the amount of stimulation required to induce stress and anxiety is increased. Less stress and anxiety means greater confidence, better performance and reduced conflict with others. Greater confidence, better performance and reduced conflict with others assist in maintaining arousal at optimum levels and increased resilience.

In addition, playing music while children sleep might also be considered to provide a focus of attention for the sleeping child's brain. It is generally accepted that having a focus for one's thoughts, such as occurs with meditation practices, is calming. So what we are doing when we play soothing classical music all night, every night in a child's sleeping environment is providing one source of noise for the brain to focus on and pay attention to.

In effect, we are training the brain to focus on one source of noise. In my home I have used this intervention on a long-term basis for the management of my middle son's tendency to quickly become overwhelmed by noise in his environment. His sensitivity to noise stems from his confirmed diagnosis of Auditory Processing Disorder. Children who suffer from this disorder have trouble paying attention to the sounds they need to listen to while ignoring other sounds. They find environments where there is more than one source of noise highly distracting and frequently overwhelming. Their brains are literally bombarded by noise. Interestingly, the original proponent of the Mozart Effect, Albert A. Tomatis[23], wrote of the virtue of music in the treatment of auditory processing problems, as well as dyslexia, learning disabilities, attention deficit disorders, autism, and sensory integration and motor-skill difficulties. Since using this intervention with my son he is calmer, happier, and his school has ceased to report concerns with his learning. Of further interest, my eldest son, who sleeps in a nearby bedroom, has asked that the music be played louder as it 'helps him sleep'.

My own experiences at home and in my practice supports Tomatis' assertions about the benefits of music in the treatment of a range of childhood difficulties, though my opinion is that the benefit is gained from the reduction of stress (arousal) associated with living with these conditions. In my practice I routinely offer caregivers who consult me about children a CD of soothing classical music to be quietly played all night, every night in the child's bedroom. Some parents are dubious about the worth of such an intervention and never try it. The vast majority of those who do try the intervention report that their child goes to sleep more quickly, sleeps more soundly and peacefully, has few, if any, nightmares, awakens happier, and is calmer, more tolerant of frustrations and challenges, and less prone to engaging in conflict with others during the day.

The above discussion of the use of music to achieve desired states of arousal alerts us to the role of the child's environment in influencing and maintaining states of arousal. In my home we have a study that is furnished something like a galley kitchen, with a long desktop along one wall. On this desktop there are three computers; one for each of my sons. The computers belonging to the eldest and youngest of my sons are at each end, with the computer belonging to my middle son in the middle. All have speakers. All are connected to the internet. From time to time all three children are on their computers, listening to music and/or playing web-based games that have background music. It can be quite a racket.

In the past, my middle son with the Auditory Processing Disorder quickly became overwhelmed by the challenge of succeeding at a web-based game against a backdrop of music from three computers. He did not cope and would exhibit emotional and behavioural outbursts. So why did we not move his computer or remove the speakers from all three computers you might ask? Both solutions would have been met with howls of 'that's unfair'. The solution, then? We plugged headphones into his computer and insisted he use them. The intention of this intervention was to limit the auditory stimulation to one source. The outcome was a much happier child and dramatically fewer emotional and behavioural outbursts while all three children were on their computers.

Certain aspects of the environment are inherently stimulating for children, such as loud and fast-paced music, computer games and background noise. Certain environments are stimulating for children, such as busy classrooms, playgrounds and shopping centres. Some children are able to tolerate being exposed to stimulating environments and environmental stimulation. Other children quickly become overwhelmed by these and display behaviours associated with elevated levels of arousal (also called *hyperarousal*) and the fight/flight/freeze response, including demanding behaviour, emotional outbursts, avoidance and withdrawal into themselves.

A walk through any busy shopping mall will provide evidence of this, with overstimulated children throwing themselves on the ground with fists bunched and arms and legs flailing, much to the embarrassment and distress of their caregivers. As caregivers, it is important to understand that this behaviour is a consequence of hyperarousal and not to exacerbate it with our own corresponding reactions of anger and frustration towards the child.

Rather, it is much more helpful to reduce the child's exposure to stimulating environments and sources of environmental stimulation and gradually re-introduce the child to them. Graded exposure to stimulation and stimulating environments, whereby the child becomes mildly over-aroused but is supported by their caregiver and removed from the environment/stimulation before they become overwhelmed, supports experiences of mastery under adverse conditions, which are important in the development of resilience.

This is all very well, but how can we assist our children to better manage their arousal levels? The capacity to self-regulate, that is, to control one's own arousal levels, has its beginnings in the first year of life. Through a process of *attunement* to the emotional state of the infant, the caregiver regulates the infant's emotional experience, ensuring that the infant does not suffer bad experiences as a result of prolonged exposure to intense emotion.

Attunement is the process where a caregiver matches their emotional state to that of their infant. In doing so, the infant and mother feel emotionally connected to each other. We know this happens, as research has shown that if you record the heart rate of mothers and their infants during play, the rise and fall of their heart rates match each other.[24] Heart rate is an indicator of arousal, and arousal is a major element of emotion, so it is thought likely that when an infant is happy, the mother feels the same or similar intensity of emotion. When the mother senses that her infant is becoming overly excited, she intervenes to calm her infant. Similarly, when their infant is distressed, a mother feels the same or similar levels of distress. She intervenes to soothe her infant, and in doing so soothes her own distress.

In regulating their infant's emotional experience, mothers also regulate the infant's *arousal*. During the second year, and as a result of an infant's caregivers consistently and effectively regulating the infant's emotional states, the infant develops the ability to regulate their own emotions,[25, 26] and hence, their arousal.

So how do we assist a child to self-regulate their arousal levels when they are older? The answer is to have them practise doing so. Engaging a child in play and games that are alternately stimulating and calming is a good way to motivate a child to engage in the process as well as achieve the desired result.

For example, you might engage a child in a vigorous game of chase or balloon volleyball and follow it up with a game like Jenga, Pick-Up Sticks, Ker-Plunk or Uno Stacko. All of these activities are fun and engaging. Chase and balloon volleyball often result in a state of high excitement and uninhibited motor movement. High excitement and uninhibited motor movement are the opposite of what is needed to perform well in Jenga, Pick-Up Sticks, Ker-Plunk and Uno Stacko. These kinds of games require calmness, concentration and a steady hand in order to succeed. Children typically try hard to calm themselves and focus in order to do well. Similarly, encouraging and supporting children to play games that require calm and focus in a noisy or otherwise stimulating environment encourages them to self-regulate their arousal levels.

Teaching children to be aware of signs in their body of what elevated levels of arousal feel like and strategies to reduce arousal are also helpful. Elevated levels of arousal can be experienced in a number of ways. Some common experiences are butterflies in the tummy, heart palpitations, sweatiness, restlessness of the arms, legs and hands, and shortness of breath. It can also be felt as muscle tension and aches and pains in almost any part of the body. The most common strategy for reducing arousal is controlled breathing. In controlled breathing, the child is taught to breathe in through the nose and out through the mouth to a three-count spanning approximately three seconds. In their mind they would typically be saying 'in-two-three-out-two-three'. In controlled breathing the child is encouraged to place their hand on their tummy and breathe in deeply, so that the tummy expands as they breathe in and contracts as they breathe out. The child might practise this activity for ten minutes at least twice per day.

Relaxation training is also helpful in teaching children how to manage their arousal levels. Relaxation training incorporates controlled breathing and follows either a tension-release method or release-only method. In tension-release, the child is encouraged to tense various muscles in their bodies for five seconds before letting them relax. In release-only, the child is encouraged to concentrate on various parts of the body and release tension from them. Tension-release is the best place to start. It is easier to grasp and is also useful in teaching children to recognize the feeling of muscle tension, a common sign of high arousal, in their body. Release-only is easier to grasp for more experienced users of relaxation training. A basic script for a caregiver to assist a child in the tension-release method is presented below.

TENSION-RELEASE

In a quiet room, sit the child down in a comfortable chair.

In a quiet, calm voice, instruct the child to slowly breathe in through their nose and out through their mouth to a three-count ('in-two-three, out-two-three') for three or four breaths.

Instruct the child to tense and relax their muscles in the following order, saying the words that are in italics. Instruct the child to tense their muscles for about five seconds and relax for about ten seconds.

Hands – *Curl your hands into fists, hold (five seconds), and then let go (ten seconds). Notice the tension as it drains away. Your hands should feel warm and heavy.*

Lower arms – *Bend your hands down at the wrist as if you are trying to touch the underside or your arms, hold, and then let go. Notice the tension as it drains away. Your arms should feel warm and heavy.*

Upper arms – *Tighten your biceps by bending your arms at the elbow, hold, and then let go. Notice the tension as it drains away. Your upper arms should feel warm and heavy.*

Shoulders – *Lift up your shoulders as if you are trying to touch your ears with them, hold, and then let go. Notice the tension as it drains away. Your shoulders should feel warm and heavy.*

Neck – *Stretch your neck gently to the left, then forward, then to the right, then to the back in a slow rolling motion, then let go. Notice the tension as it drains away. Your neck should feel warm and heavy.*

Forehead and scalp – *Raise your eyebrows, hold, and then let go. Notice the tension as it drains away. Your forehead and scalp should feel warm and heavy.*

Eyes – *Screw up your eyes, hold, and then let go. Notice the tension as it drains away. Your face should feel warm and heavy.*

Jaw – *Clench your jaw (just to tighten the muscles), hold, and then let go. Notice the tension as it drains away. Your jaw should feel warm and heavy.*

Tongue – *Press your tongue against the roof of your mouth, hold, and then let go. Notice the tension as it drains away. Your mouth should feel warm and heavy.*

Upper back – *Pull your shoulders forward with your arms at your side, hold, and then let go. Notice the tension as it drains away. Your upper back should feel warm and heavy.*

Lower back – *Roll your upper body forward at the waist in a smooth circle, tensing your lower back, and then let go. Notice the tension as it drains away. You lower back should feel warm and heavy.*

Buttocks – *Tighten your buttocks, hold, and then let go. Notice the tension as it drains away. Your buttocks should feel warm and heavy.*

Thighs – *Push your feet firmly into the floor, hold, and then let go. Notice the tension as it drains away. Your thighs should feel warm and heavy.*

Calves – *Lift your toes off the ground towards your shins, hold, then let go. Notice the tension as it drains away. Your calves should feel warm and heavy.*

Feet – *Gently curl your toes down so that they are pressing into the floor, hold, and then let go. Notice the tension as it drains away. Your feet should feel warm and heavy.*

Sit still for a few minutes and enjoy the feeling of relaxation.

Meditation practices are also useful for teaching children skills to regulate their arousal once they have been taught to recognize the signs of high arousal in their body. A simple meditation involves the child imagining that they are in their favourite place in the world; the place where they feel warm, safe, relaxed and happy. Children should be encouraged to imagine as much as possible about this setting, including what they can see, hear, smell, feel and taste when they are in their special place. Children should be encouraged to practise this meditation for ten minutes twice a day, and to use it when they become aware of signs in their body that their arousal levels are high.

Exercise is another way for children to release tension and lower their arousal levels. It is good for their health too. Children should exercise for at least 30 minutes each day. Encouraging them to walk or ride their bike to and from school is a start, safety permitting. Encouraging them to play team sports is another way to ensure they are exercising and has the added benefit of promoting positive socialization. Owning a pet can be soothing for children; having a dog that requires a daily walk can be a further means of ensuring that children exercise.

In addition, children feel safe, and hence less over-aroused and anxious in an environment where adults provide consistent, sensitive and responsive care, where daily routines and family rituals are established and maintained, and where expectations regarding behaviour are known, consistent and sensitively implemented. A sense of order and predictability are important in minimizing uncertainty, and its effect, anxiety. This is often highlighted in the behaviour of many school-aged children on weekends and during school holidays. Many children exhibit a propensity to become unsettled when weekends and school holidays are unstructured or deviate significantly from the school-day routine. Parents often comment that their children miss the routine of attending school and are 'ready' to return by the end of longer holiday periods. Unsettled children benefit from their caregivers maintaining daily routines, such as bedtime, rising time, and mealtimes, and making known to the child as much as possible of what will occur on weekends and during school holiday periods. In doing so the purpose is not to eliminate all unstructured time, but to ensure that the child is as prepared as they can be to manage such times.

Children also experience comfort and reassurance and, hence, lower levels of arousal, when their caregivers are competent, knowing, caring and accessible. Children need to be able to rely on their caregivers to help them when they feel overwhelmed. This means that caregivers should intervene to soothe their children when they are in physical and emotional distress.

The knowledge that their parent is there for them and can and will intervene should the child feel overwhelmed provides powerful encouragement for children to accept challenges and face up to conditions of adversity. Anticipating the child's needs and wishes is one way in which a caregiver shows the child that they are knowing and caring. When caregivers attend to children and provide for them before the child does anything to make it happen, the child has a powerful experience that the caregiver is thinking of them, is aware of their needs and reasonable wishes, and is willing to respond to these without the child having to go to great lengths to obtain a caregiving response. Children take comfort from these experiences. Verbalizing understanding of the child's thoughts, feelings, wishes and intentions is another way a caregiver shows the child that they are knowing and caring. Verbalizing understanding is discussed in detail in the next chapter.

Directing children rather than asking them to perform tasks reinforces adult authority, as does avoiding fighting battles the child might win. Instead of asking a child 'can you pick up that block please?', you might simply say 'pick up that block please' or 'please pick up that block'. When you ask a child to perform a task you effectively give them a choice about whether to do it or not. If they refuse to perform the task and you end up directing them to do it, the child feels resentful, a battle might follow and parental authority is undermined. Directing children reinforces the right of adults to direct children. Battles might occur, so adults need to be careful not to be unreasonable about what they direct the child to do. Directing children in simple tasks where compliance is likely gets children used to being directed. Finally, taking responsibility for important decisions that affect a child's life is another means by which parental authority is reinforced. This includes decisions regarding the child's schooling, what movies they can watch, their movements and the management of health or developmental issues affecting the child. Where this does not occur children invariably experience anxiety.

This is poignantly illustrated by the experiences of children whose residential arrangements following parental separation are determined by law courts. In my work I am frequently referred children whose parents have separated. Typically, the presenting problem is emotional and/or behavioural problems that might be attributed to anxiety. Often there is residual enmity between the parents. Commonly, the children, feeling insecure about how the people they love can stop loving each other and worrying that they may themselves become unloved, seek to reassure each parent of their devotion to them by asserting that they want to spend more time with them.

A protracted custody battle may have already occurred, with the result that a judge is forced to resolve the issue of the child's residence; often to the dissatisfaction of both parents. Even where an outcome is agreed to with the support of a third party mediator, parents of children often feel as though they were forced into reaching a settlement. So what do they tell their child when he or she asks to spend more time with them and less time with the other parent? They say that they wish that they could make this happen but the judge (or the other parent, solicitor, mediator, family assessor) won't let them. Suddenly, the child feels like their parent no longer has any say over what happens in their life. Rather than being the most powerful person in their life, their parents are subject to the authority of others. Naturally, this is anxiety-evoking for these children.

In these circumstances, the child benefits from the parent acknowledging the child's possible motivations for asking to spend more time with them, but reinforcing that the outcome is a parental decision, even if they, the parent, are not happy with it. To simply attribute blame for the decision to others and express helplessness to change it weakens the prestige in which the parent is held by the child and undermines the child's resilience.

CHAPTER SUMMARY

- Arousal refers to the level of activity of the body's nervous systems.

- Arousal goes up and down during the day, depending on our mood, what we are doing, and what is happening in our environment.

- Arousal generally is lowest when we are asleep and highest when we are in a state of high emotion.

- Each person's range of arousal varies as a result of genetic inheritance, early exposure to stress, ongoing maintaining factors, and the interaction of these.

- We need to be aroused to a certain level in order to perform at our best. When arousal is too low, or too high, our best performance is not possible.

- Arousal might be thought of as a gauge of resilience, much like a thermometer is a gauge of body temperature.

- High levels of arousal are associated with anxiety problems in children.

- Anxiety impacts negatively on a child's capacity to perform at his or her best and experience mastery.

- Mastery experiences are critical to the development of beliefs about self-worth and potency that are beneficial to the individual and enhance resilience.

- Optimal arousal for mastery and resilience can be achieved with interventions that address:

  o the child's environment

  o experience of caregiving, and

  o ability to self-regulate their arousal levels.

CHAPTER 3

PSYCHOLOGICAL INFLUENCES – ATTACHMENT

There is nothing either good or bad, but thinking makes it so.[27]
(Shakespeare, *Hamlet*, Act II, Scene II)

Consider which of the following children is most likely to be the resilient one:

1. the child who is always telling others how good he is
2. the one who complains that he is no good at anything, or
3. the child who says very little about what he is good at and not good at?

Then think about which of these other children is most likely to be the resilient one:

1. the child who never asks for help when trying something new
2. the one who is always asking for help when trying something new, or
3. the child who sometimes asks for help when trying something new?

The answer to both questions is the third child. The reason lies in our understanding of *attachment* and the influence it has over the way in which children think about themselves, others and their world.

So what is attachment? Attachment is the term used for the special relationship children develop towards their primary caregivers during infancy. It is special because these are the people the infant learns to trust and depend upon to look after them. It is also special because infants expect other adults in a caregiving role to be like their primary caregivers. That is, attachment relationships formed in infancy directly influence the child's expectations about all other interactions and relationships with others.

Primary caregivers are the people who provide day-to-day care to the child during infancy. Primary caregivers are usually mothers and fathers, though they can also include relatives and regular child carers; in fact, anyone who provides physical and emotional care on a continuous and consistent basis.

Primary caregivers towards whom a child forms an attachment are called 'attachment figures'. A child's attachment to their attachment figures incorporates feelings of emotional connectedness and an expectation that these people can be depended upon to support them in their efforts, respond to their needs and keep them safe from harm.

Attachment is most obvious in the child's preference for their attachment figures over other available adults for interaction and a caregiving response when they are uncertain, in need and in distress, and in the responsiveness of the child to interaction and caregiving from their attachment figures. Though their attachments do not rule out acceptance of caregiving from other available adults, a child is more likely to be successfully soothed when they are distressed, and to accept caregiving when they are in need, from their attachment figures. Where an attachment figure is not present, the quality of the attachment relationship influences the child's interactions and acceptance of caregiving from other available adults.

As mentioned in Chapter 1, a child's attachment to his or her caregivers is an important contributor to resilience. This is because the quality of attachment relationships strongly influences the child's beliefs regarding their competency and worth, the sensitivity and responsiveness of others and the safety and providence of their world. In turn, these perceptions directly influence the child's capacity and willingness to explore their environment, take risks, accept challenges and cope with failure.

Children are not born attached to their primary caregivers. Attachment relationships emerge over time and as a result of interactions between the child and his or her primary caregiver(s). These interactions, and the child's resultant attachment to their primary caregivers, typically begin in the first year of life and develop progressively over the first four years of life.

From birth to three months the infant orients to the sound of the caregiver's voice and tracks the carer visually, but smiling and reaching to be held are considered to be reflexes and indiscriminate.[28, 29, 30] Between three and eight months of age the infant begins to recognize their primary caregivers and discriminate them from other adults. By eight months of age the infant demonstrates a clear preference for their primary caregivers and a corresponding wariness towards strangers.

Whereas they might previously have been happy to be passed around between various friends and relatives for a cuddle and a hold, from about eight months of age the infant prefers to be cuddled and held by the primary caregivers. Similarly, from about eight months of age the infant prefers the primary caregivers to respond to their dependency needs, such as feeding, changing, bathing, and soothing when they are distressed. That is, in ordinary circumstances the infant shows clear evidence of having learnt that they can trust and depend on their primary caregivers by eight months of age. Given that the infant is preverbal at this time, and hence cannot be instructed as to who their primary caregivers are, the formation of attachment relationships is based on their *experiences* of relatedness with the primary caregivers.

So what does an infant *experience* in their relationship with their primary caregiver that facilitates the development of attachment? The first aspect of their experience is that their caregiver is a recurring feature of their day-to-day life. Even when they are not actually physically present, the caregiver repeatedly returns to the infant. Hence, by one means of another the caregiver is *accessible* to the infant.[31]

A second aspect of the infant's experience is that their primary caregiver feeds them when they are hungry, burps them when they have stomach pain, changes their nappy when it is dirty and uncomfortable, soothes them when they are distressed and engages with them when they are seeking interaction. That is, the infant experiences their caregiver as *understanding* and *responsive.*[32] In association with this the infant learns that they can trust and depend on their caregivers.

A third aspect of the infant's experience, related to the last, is that when they are distressed their caregiver is distressed too. The infant notices this in the facial expressions and movements of their caregiver. As the caregiver soothes the infant, the caregiver also soothes themself. Their face and body relaxes and they become smooth and coordinated in their motor movements, including their rocking of the infant. Similarly, when the infant smiles and laughs in association with feelings of pleasure, their caregiver also smiles and laughs. At other times the caregiver smiles at the infant, engendering feelings of pleasure in the infant. In this way, the infant begins to feel emotionally connected to their caregiver.

Support for this process is reflected in research, described earlier, which shows that heart rate curves (an indicator of arousal, and hence, emotion) of infants and mothers parallel each other during play.[33] We refer to this process where the infant's caregiver matches the emotional state of their infant as *attunement*.

As referred to above, in the context of their day-to-day interactions with their attachment figures, children form enduring beliefs or 'working models' about their competency and worth, the sensitivity and responsiveness of others and the safety and providence of their world. Attachment theorists call these beliefs or working models *Attachment Representations*.[34, 35, 36] Where attachment figures are consistently *accessible* to the infant, consistently demonstrate *understanding* of the child's signals regarding their needs and *responsiveness* to these needs, and where attachment figures are consistently *attuned* to the child's emotional state and regulate the child's emotional experience, the child typically forms positive attachment representations regarding their competency and worth, the sensitivity and responsiveness of others, and the safety and providence of their world.

Where attachment figures are inconsistently accessible, understanding, responsive, and attuned, or where there is inconsistency across attachment figures, the child is likely to be unsure about what to expect of themselves, others and their world, resulting in anxiety and compulsive attempts to reassure themselves regarding caregiver accessibility, understanding and responsiveness. Children whose attachment figures are *consistently* accessible, understanding, responsive, and attuned are typically found to exhibit *secure* attachments.[37] Children whose attachment figures provide inconsistent care are typically found to exhibit *insecure* attachments.[38, 39] Although estimates vary, research indicates that approximately 65 per cent of children in Western countries are securely attached to their primary caregiver or caregivers.[40]

Securely attached children hold positive beliefs about their competency and worth, the sensitivity and responsiveness of others and the safety and providence of their world. As a result, they are more likely to hold and maintain positive beliefs in the face of adversity, to accept challenges and to cope with failure. They are more likely to think realistically about their abilities and to confidently explore their world without the debilitating and restricting effects of worries about competence, safety and accessibility of caring adults. Through confident exploration of their world and acceptance of risks and challenges, securely attached children are more likely to experience mastery, thereby reinforcing their positive attachment representations.

If we return to my questions at the start of this chapter about who is most likely to be the resilient child, the child who is always telling others how good he is seems to be preoccupied with receiving the approval of others. I suspect that he in fact has doubts about his own abilities and about whether others, including adults in a caregiving role, will notice him. Similarly, the child who complains that he is no good at anything seems preoccupied with obtaining caregiver assistance. Both of these children seem to be insecure. In contrast, the child who says very little about what he is good at and not good at seems to be comfortable with his abilities and with the likelihood that adults in a caregiving role will notice him and assist him where required. He is more likely to be a secure child. Similarly, the child who never asks for help and the child who always asks for help when trying something new might be seen to hold unhelpful beliefs and worries about the accessibility and responsiveness of adults in a caregiving role and their own deservedness. In contrast, the child who sometimes asks for help might be seen to exhibit confidence in their ability to give it a go and the knowledge that if it gets too hard adults are prepared and able to lend a hand.

So, if it is desirable, in terms of enhancing their resilience, for children to be securely attached to their primary caregivers and to hold secure attachment representations, how do we ensure that children remain securely attached to their primary caregivers and maintain positive representations regarding their competency and worth, the sensitivity and responsiveness of others, and the safety and providence of their world? In addition, how do we improve the quality of attachment relationships and promote positive attachment representations among insecure children?

Fortunately, children integrate new information and experiences into their overall attachment status and associated attachment representations.[41] It follows that by influencing the child's experience of relatedness with others we can enhance attachment security. As the quality of attachment relationships is heavily influenced by the child's experiences of caregiver accessibility, understanding, responsiveness and affective attunement, it follows that attachment security can be enhanced through enrichment of the child's experiences in these key areas.

PROMOTING AND PRESERVING ATTACHMENT SECURITY

Enriching caregiver understanding

Implicit in the task of enriching caregiver understanding is the concept that nobody ever does anything for no reason. That is, whatever behaviour a child is exhibiting there is always a reason for the child doing so.

Some reasons are obvious, such as the child who is hungry asking for food. Others are not so obvious, such as the child who has just eaten a large meal asking for some snack food.

In this latter example, the adult in a caregiving role might easily overlook the possibility that the child is seeking reassurance that their siblings do not eat all of the snack foods available before the child who is requesting a snack gets a chance to have their share. As a result of their failure to understand this and concern that their child might develop unhealthy eating habits and become overweight, the adult may well say no to this request. Under such circumstances, the child is likely to feel as though the adult has not heard or understood them and to become increasingly worried or anxious about accessing what they perceive to be their fair share. In order to manage their worries, the child may make persistent requests, resulting in parental frustration and anger, or sneak off with the snack food; the latter also resulting in parental anger and frustration upon discovery, and likely also in a further restriction of the child's access to snack food.

In either event, the child's relationship with their care-giver is not enhanced, with the result that they are more likely to be concerned about their ability to influence the caregiving behaviour of the adult, and the likelihood that the adult will understand their needs and wishes in future. In contrast, were the caregiver to respond with understanding, acknowledging the child's fears about missing out and setting aside the child's share of the available snack food while also declining the child's request, the child is more likely to feel reassured that their caregiver understands them, thereby reducing their worry and maintaining and strengthening secure attachment representations.

Responding with understanding is easier when the child has exhibited socially acceptable behaviour and more difficult when the child has exhibited behaviour that is not sociably accepted. However, given that all children display behaviour that is not socially accepted at least some of the time, unless caregivers respond with understanding in both circumstances the child is likely to experience their caregiver as inconsistent in their understanding and responsiveness. The result of such inconsistency is that the child might feel unsure of their capacity to secure a caregiving response, their deservedness of such a response, and the sensitivity and responsiveness of others. That is, inconsistency of caregiver understanding and responsiveness gives rise to insecurity.

In order to avoid promoting and maintaining attachment insecurity it is useful to have an understanding of how beliefs and attitudes develop and are maintained. In psychology, one of the most influential schools of thought is the cognitive-behavioural school. Implicit in cognitive-behavioural formulations of the way beliefs and attitudes develop and are maintained is the idea that the way an individual thinks about or judges themself, others and their social world influences how they feel. Their feelings, in turn, influence how they behave. Their behaviour plays a key role in how others respond to them. The response of others is typically consistent with the original thought, thus confirming in the mind of the individual the validity of that thought. A conventional term that might be seen as reflecting this process is self-fulfilling prophecies, and is represented in Figure 3.1.[42]

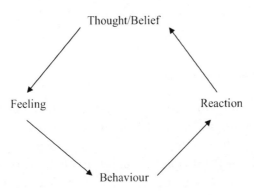

Figure 3.1 Self-fulfilling prophecy

A self-fulfilling prophecy common to the experience of children is represented in Figure 3.2. In response to a caregiver disciplining a child for unacceptable behaviour without pausing to consider the reasons why the child has engaged in the behaviour, the child thinks that the adult does not understand and is being mean and unfair. The thought that the adult is mean and unfair precipitates feelings of anger. In association with their anger, the child yells, hits or breaks objects. The adult further reprimands and disciplines the child for yelling, hitting or breaking objects, thus confirming for the child the original thought that adults are mean and unfair. As this process is repeated over time, the original thought becomes a belief.

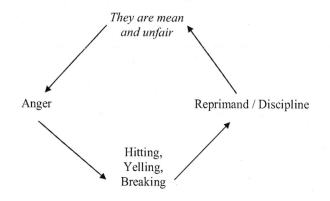

Figure 3.2 A self-fulfilling prophecy

In order to promote and support more positive beliefs about self, others and world, adults who interact with children in a caregiving role need to circumvent this process of confirming and reinforcing unhelpful thoughts and beliefs. While some advocate intervening in the area of the child's thoughts, feelings and/or behaviour, I advocate intervening in the area of the response of the adult to the behaviour of the child. In view of the crucial part it plays in soothing the infant and encouraging trusting dependency on adults in a caregiving role, it is important to respond with *understanding*, as represented in Figure 3.3.

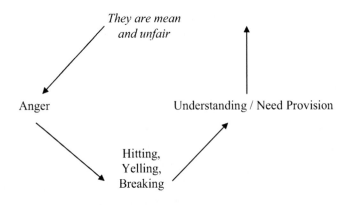

Figure 3.3 Circumventing self-fulfilling prophecies

To respond with understanding protects against reinforcing unhelpful beliefs about oneself and adults in a caregiving role. Responding to the need as well as the behaviour is one method by which an adult in a caregiving role can respond with understanding. Nearly all human behaviour has a function and purpose and children rarely misbehave for misbehaviour's sake. Among other things, misbehaviour can serve as an emotional release (such as when children are tired and over aroused) or as a strategy to draw attention to an unmet need. Maladjusted and pre-verbal children are typically unable or unwilling to express their needs directly/verbally and do so through controlling and manipulative behaviours. From their first day, infants draw attention to their needs through affective displays that might later come to be viewed as developmentally inappropriate and socially unacceptable. Nevertheless, they have learnt that crying and screaming is an effective way to draw parental attention. It is not surprising that this broadens to other unacceptable behaviours among toddlers, such as throwing objects, banging doors, turning the TV and lights off and on, and so on. Naughty behaviour typically attracts more attention than good behaviour. When a child is misbehaving it is important to try and work out what unexpressed need might be giving rise to the behaviour rather than simply responding to the behaviour alone. Thereafter, it is important to respond to the need as well as the behaviour. Responding to the need as well as the behaviour is soothing for the child, it reinforces for the child that their caregiver is understanding and responsive, and it is helpful in preserving and promoting secure attachment representations. This process of responding to the need as well as the behaviour is exemplified in Table 3.1.

Another powerful way to create an experience of understanding is to say out loud what you think the child is thinking or feeling and what their intentions are/were, for there is always a reason why the child has acted in the way that they have.

I call this *verbalizing understanding*. For example, if a child strikes out at another child in the classroom, it is useful to pause and consider that the child may well have done so because they were angry at something the other child did and that they did not think that the teacher would notice or care enough to intervene. The child may also have been raised in an environment where physicality is an accepted manner of expressing anger. In contrast to simply disciplining the child who hit out, thereby confirming their belief that they are bad and unsafe and adults are uncaring, verbalizing understanding gets around this process by providing the child with the experience that their feelings and intentions are understood and important. This is soothing to the child and lays the foundations for a relationship based on trust and secure dependency;[43] just as occurs in the infant-caregiver interactions. When used routinely it also facilitates opportunities to manage behaviour effectively. What do I mean by verbalizing understanding to facilitate opportunities that manage behaviour effectively? Well, have you ever had the experience that you might as well be talking to the wall when disciplining a child? This common experience arises when the child who is being disciplined appears not to be taking in what the adult is saying.

There are at least two very real reasons why the child appears to be ignoring what is being said to them. The first reason is that they are determined not to engage. The second reason is that they cannot. With regard to the first reason, it is important to consider that *in order to be heard we first need to listen.* That is, a child is more likely to pay attention to what the adult in a caregiving role is saying to them if they feel as though the adult has taken time to listen to, acknowledge and understand their perspective first. The second reason stems from the way in which our brain works when we are distressed. Brain imaging studies show that when an individual is under stress the blood flow moves from the outer part of the brain to the inner part of the brain.[44, 45]

The outer part of the brain, or cerebral cortex, is responsible for logical, rational thinking, planning and responding. The inner part of the brain is responsible for instinctive responses that are essential to the survival of the organism, such as respiration, arousal, body temperature and emotion. When a child is in distress their ability to think and reason logically is reduced. If they are distressed enough, their ability to think and reason logically is almost non-existent. Hence, you really might as well talk to the wall! So what is the alternative? In order to discipline effectively one needs to reduce the child's fear and distress. What is one of the most powerful means by which to reduce a child's distress? Verbalizing understanding. Table 3.2 provides examples of how to verbalize understanding in response to behaviours typically displayed by children, and effective management responses that are implemented *after* verbalizing understanding.

Table 3.1 Responding to the need as well as the behaviour

Behaviour	Possible explanation	Need	Helpful responses	Unhelpful responses
Child refuses to stay in their bed at night time.	Separation anxiety and/or insecurity.	Reassurance that the care-giver is aware of them, accessible and responsive.	Remain calm. Engage in soothing bedtime rituals (e.g. reading and singing to child). Checking back in with the child before they get out of bed to achieve physical closeness to the caregiver (see 'emotional refuelling in reverse' on p.69)	Parental anger and frustration. Disciplining the child. Ignoring the child.
Child refuses to eat their food.	Child does not like the taste of the food or its texture (i.e. they may be tactile sensitive).	Food that is nutritious tastes good and feels good on the palate.	Remain calm. Prepare nutritious meals that are to the child's taste. Seek advice from an occupational therapist who specializes in sensory integration difficulties and a dietician who specializes in children's diet.	Parental anger and frustration. Making the child remain seated until they have eaten all of the food. Threats and consequences for noncompliance.
Child becomes overly loud and boisterous at a family function.	Child is overstimulated.	Soothing and/or opportunities to blow off steam.	Temporarily withdrawing the child from the stimulating environment in order to calm/soothe them or provide them with a release.	Yelling at the child to 'calm down'.
Child 'shuts down' in class.	Child is overstimulated.	Reduce stress.	Understanding and soothing.	Threatening and punishing.

Table 3.2 Verbalizing understanding

Behaviour	Possible reason	Example of an unhelpful or ineffective response	Example of an understanding response	Example of an effective management response
Child sneaks snack food from cupboard.	Hungry.	Admonishment and restriction of access to food.	*I think you must have been hungry.*	Make it a rule that the child must ask for snacks.
	Concerned siblings will eat first.		*I think you were worried that your brother and sister might eat them all before you did.*	Make it a rule that the child must ask for snacks and divide the available snacks into separate containers for each child of the household.
Child hits another child.	Other child hit first.	Anger and disapproval	*They must have done something to make you feel really angry.*	*Next time someone does something that makes you angry you should…* (desired behaviour)
Child behaving in a loud and boisterous manner.	Overstimulated.	Raising your voice and speaking to them in terms of threats and consequences (e.g. *if you don't calm down this minute…*)	*I think that you are very excited.*	Reduce stimulation or provide opportunities to blow off steam.

Behaviour	Underlying cause	Unhelpful response	Helpful verbal response	Helpful strategy
Child runs out of the classroom.	Anxiety.	Chasing the child and demanding that they remain in the classroom. Disciplining the child for not remaining in the classroom.	*You must have felt really scared in there.*	Developing strategies for assisting the child to feel safe in the classroom.
Child refuses to go to bed.	Separation anxiety.	Demanding that the child remain in bed and threatening them with consequences if they do not.	*You must be really worried that I won't hear you if you need me.*	Soothing bedtime rituals (e.g. reading and singing to child). Emotional refuelling in reverse (see p.69).
Child answers back to an adult.	Child feels the adult has not understood or heard their point of view.	Admonishing the child for being rude.	*You think that I do not understand. You think that I do not listen to you.*	Respond with understanding, make it clear that answering back is not acceptable behaviour, and identify the consequences of future instances of answering back to adults.

Enriching caregiver accessibility

In addition to getting around the process of maintaining and strengthening insecure attachment representations, verbalizing understanding regarding accessibility to needs-provision reassures children that the adult in a caregiving role is aware of them and understands their needs and wishes. It provides an experience that is similar to what an infant experiences when their caregiver notices when they are hungry and feeds them. Statements that communicate understanding of accessibility worries include the following:[46]

- I think that you believe that I will forget about you if we are not always together.

- I think that you believe I won't notice or understand when you really need me/something.

- You believe that if I don't do it [get it for you] now I will forget.

- You worry that I won't come back for you.

- You worry that I don't like you anymore.

- You know you have done something wrong and you worry that I won't like/love you anymore.

My own experiences at home and in my practice have shown me that such statements reduce children's anxiety and associated obsessions and compulsive attempts to reassure themselves about accessibility to needs-provision.

Another way in which adults in a caregiving role can reassure the child about accessibility to needs-provision is based on the infant's experience of the accessibility of their caregivers. From approximately eight months of age the infant develops the capacity to move about their environment. Once they can do so, secure infants will begin to explore their environment while also seeking temporary reunions with their preferred caregivers for *emotional refuelling*. Emotional refuelling incorporates the infant approaching the caregiver and the caregiver attending to the infant, thereby alleviating the infant's emerging anxiety at having been separated from their caregiver. In association with repeated experiences of temporary separations, reunions and emotional refuelling, secure infants develop an appreciation of the fact that their caregivers are aware of them, accessible and responsive, without having to be with their caregiver all of the time.

Applied to the older child, adults in a caregiving role would seek out the child to physically and emotionally make contact before the child seeks out the caregiver or otherwise takes some action to command the caregiver's attention. Referred to by me[47] as *emotional refuelling in reverse*, this strategy enables children to have experiences of adults in a caregiving role being aware of them and responding to them without the child having to do something to make it so, thereby promoting and maintaining positive expectations of adults in a caregiving role and their own deservedness of a caregiving response.

Enriching caregiver attunement: Empathy

A related concept to responding with understanding is responding with empathy. A common way of thinking about empathy is that it involves the capacity to see, feel and acknowledge things from the perspective of another person. Most adults in a caregiving role consider themselves to be empathic towards children in their care, and the fact is they are, most of the time. But consider the example of the child who has fallen over and scraped their knee. Examination of the knee reveals a very minor scrape and almost no bleeding. Yet, the child is in considerable distress, crying and asserting how much it hurts. How do you respond?

Many adults, seeking to make the child feel better, will respond with something like 'It's okay; it is only a little scratch'. In doing so, they are trying to reassure the child that nothing terrible has happened or likely to happen. How does the child respond to this? Well, it varies. Some children become less demonstrative and are likely to be less demonstrative in similar instances in future. Other children become even more demonstrative and demanding of a caregiving response. What is the problem here? The problem is that reassurance is not the same as empathy. Reassurance alone does not ensure that the child feels understood and that their pain is valid. In fact, reassurance alone ensures that the child does not feel understood and validated. The result is that the child feels undeserving and unable to secure the understanding response that they crave and/or perceives adults as not understanding or caring. Their lack of demonstrative behaviour or disproportionate distress under similar circumstances in future reflects the fact that they do not feel confident of receiving the caregiving response they desire.

Contrast this with the scenario where the adult in the caregiving role expresses concern that is proportional to the distress being exhibited by the child. Exclaiming over how much such an injury would hurt, the adult gently cleans and bandages it. The child feels understood and an emotional union with the adult in a caregiving role. They feel able to influence the responsiveness of others and deserving of care. They perceive that adults are understanding and responsive. Ironically, an adult's original intention to reassure a child is best achieved by responding with understanding and empathy.

In addition to responding with empathy, engaging with children one-to-one in mutually enjoyable activities, commonly referred to as 'special time', is an important component in the promotion of secure attachment representations. Mimicking the playful and loving interactions between mother/father and infant, special time facilitates experiences of emotional connectedness and opportunities for the adult in a caregiving role to shape and manage the child's affective experience, such as is apparent during the playful encounters of mother and infant.[48] When scheduled on a regular and predictable basis it reassures the child regarding the accessibility of adults in a caregiving role. It reassures the child that they are important and delighted in, thereby promoting positive representations regarding self and others.

CHAPTER SUMMARY

- Attachment is the term used for the special relationship children develop towards their primary caregivers during infancy.

- Primary caregivers are the people who provide day-to-day care to the child during infancy.

- Primary caregivers towards whom a child forms an attachment are called attachment figures.

- A child's attachment to their attachment figures incorporates feelings of emotional connectedness and an expectation that their attachment figures can be depended upon to support them in their efforts, respond to their needs and keep them safe from harm.

- Where an attachment figure is not present, the quality of the attachment relationship influences the child's interactions and acceptance of caregiving from other available adults.

- Quality of attachment relationships strongly influences the child's beliefs regarding their competency and worth, the sensitivity and responsiveness of others, and the safety and providence of their world.

- Attachment relationships formed in infancy directly influence the child's expectations about all other interactions and relationships with others.

- These expectations directly influence the child's capacity and willingness to explore their environment, take risks, accept challenges and cope with failure.

- Children are not born attached to their primary caregivers. Attachment relationships emerge over time and as a result of interactions between the child and his or her primary caregiver(s) and their experiences of caregiver accessibility, understanding and attunement.

- In the context of their day-to-day interactions with their attachment figures, children form enduring beliefs or 'working models' about their competency and worth, the sensitivity and responsiveness of others and the safety and providence of their world. Attachment theorists call these beliefs or working models Attachment Representations.

- Where attachment figures are consistently accessible to the infant, consistently demonstrate understanding of the child's signals regarding their needs and responsiveness to these needs, and where attachment figures are consistently attuned to the child's emotional state and regulate the child's emotional experience, the child typically forms positive attachment representations regarding their competency and worth, the sensitivity and responsiveness of others and the safety and providence of their world.

- Where attachment figures are inconsistently accessible, understanding, responsive, and attuned, or where there is inconsistency across attachment figures, the child is likely to be unsure about what to expect of themselves, others and their world. This results in anxiety and compulsive attempts to reassure themselves regarding caregiver accessibility, understanding and responsiveness.

- Children who hold positive attachment representations are referred to as being securely attached.

- Securely attached children hold positive beliefs about their competency and worth, the sensitivity and responsiveness of others and the safety and providence of their world.

- Securely attached children are more likely to hold and maintain positive beliefs in the face of adversity, to accept challenges and to cope with failure.

- Securely attached children are more likely to think realistically about their abilities and to confidently explore their world without the debilitating and restricting effects of worries about competence, safety and accessibility of caring adults.

- Through confident exploration of their world and acceptance of risks and challenges, securely attached children are more likely to experience mastery, thereby reinforcing their positive attachment representations.

- Attachment security can be enhanced with interventions that target:
  o caregiver understanding
  o caregiver accessibility
  o caregiver attunement.

CHAPTER **4**

ENVIRONMENTAL INFLUENCES – NEEDS-PROVISION

Why do infants form attachments to their primary caregivers? Why do children learn to conform to expected standards of behaviour in a given society or culture? Why do adults seek out intimate relationships? What function does it serve to engage in these pursuits? Why do we do anything? The answer to all of these questions has to do with our needs and the satisfaction of them.

Infants form attachments because attachment relationships meet their need to be loved, cared for and kept safe from harm. Children conform to standards of expected behaviour in order to get along with others and to enhance their prospects of being loved, accepted, cared for and protected.

Adults seek out intimate relationships for love, acceptance, companionship and reproduction. All behaviour and intentions have a purpose. The purpose of our behaviour is to access needs-provision and/or enhance our prospects of doing so. Being able to get our needs met is a source of emotional well-being. When difficulties are encountered in getting our needs met we feel anxious and become preoccupied with the need. A preoccupation with needs limits our capacity to have full and satisfying life experiences. As mentioned in Chapter 1, in order for children to achieve their developmental potential and lead a full and satisfying life, they need to believe that they are able to satisfy needs that are essential to their survival and happiness. The love, care, acceptance and protection of an adult caregiver who is thought of as better able to cope with the world are examples of needs that, when consistently met, ensure that children survive and thrive. Shelter and physical sustenance are also important needs that must be met.

In the absence of reliable satisfaction of the needs which are essential to their survival and happiness, children become anxious. Their anxiety activates the parts of the brain that control instinctive survival responses and de-activates those parts of the brain that are responsible for logical thinking, planning, and action.[49] When this occurs children become demanding and difficult to reason with. They are typically resistant to having their attention diverted elsewhere. Continued denial of their attempts to get their needs satisfied often results in an escalation of their anxiety. Gaining satisfaction of their needs becomes the most important objective in the child's life in that moment – an apparent matter of survival.

The result is that the child displays a restricted range of interest and behaviour until their needs are consistently met. This restricted range of interest and behaviour limits the child's capacity to live life to the full and perform daily tasks. This is most obvious among maltreated children who, having been denied consistent access to sensitive and loving care, exhibit a limited range of interests and a proneness to engage in controlling and manipulative patterns of relating to others, particularly towards adults in a caregiving role, in order to reassure themselves that they have access to their needs.

To give an example from my own experience, I have observed my children become anxious, unreasonably demanding and resistant to redirection as a result of the demands of running a family business, which cause my wife and me to be preoccupied and less accessible to the children from time to time. Though their demands may involve something as simple as having one of us play a game with them or to have us fix them a snack, their real need is for our time and attention.

Similarly, a child who needs to be reassured that they are loved may be unreasonably demanding of affection. It is important to remember that important needs are often expressed as simple requests and wishes. It is also important to consider that in the denial of simple requests and wishes we may be denying the child fulfilment of an important need. This is where responding to our children with understanding, as described in the previous chapter, is so important.

Consistently demonstrating understanding and responding to our children's real needs, including their need for our love, attention, acceptance and protection, is reassuring to our children. Once reassured that they can rely on us to consistently respond to their needs, our children can get on with exploring all that their world offers without experiencing the debilitating and restricting effects of anxiety. By reducing anxiety and facilitating opportunities for exploration and mastery, reliable and consistent needs-provision is a potent resiliency factor.

I've mentioned consistency a lot, but why is it so important? An answer can be found in famous research studies conducted by the psychologist, B.F. Skinner. During the 1930s, Skinner developed an apparatus to study learning behaviour in laboratory animals. Referred to as the *Skinner Box*, this box-like apparatus incorporated a lever or bar, and a chute. Rats were placed in the Skinner Box and exposed to three conditions. In the first condition, a pellet of food was delivered via the chute each time the rat pressed the bar or lever. This condition was referred to as *continuous reinforcement*. The rats quickly learnt that by pressing the bar or lever they would receive food. In the second condition, a food pellet was delivered inconsistently, such as on the first, third or fourth press of the bar or lever.

This condition was referred to as *intermittent reinforcement*. The rats learnt more slowly that by pressing the bar food would be delivered. In the third condition no food was delivered through the chute, no matter how many times the rat pressed the bar or lever. The rats in the first condition appeared to press the bar or lever when they required food. The rats in the third condition soon stopped pressing the bar. Now this is the important bit. The rats in the second condition pressed the bar persistently, even after food was no longer delivered in association with presses of the bar or lever, in an apparent attempt to reassure themselves that they could access food.

Like the rats in Skinner's experiments, children who experience inconsistent caregiving become preoccupied or obsessed with their needs and with securing a response to them. As with most preoccupations and obsessions, there are associated compulsive behaviours. Because the child is experiencing anxiety in relation to their need not being met, their compulsive behaviours might be viewed as a survival response.

As mentioned earlier, survival responses are not generated by the part of the brain that controls logical thinking, planning and responding. They are controlled by the part of the brain that is concerned with taking whatever action is necessary in order to ensure the person's survival. The child acts in a manner that appears unreasonable because the part of the brain that controls reasonable thinking and action has been turned off. Typically, caregivers become preoccupied with addressing the child's 'unreasonable' behaviour and emotional displays, with the result that the need continues to go unmet and anxiety is heightened. A more effective way to reduce or eliminate unreasonable, demanding, obsessive behaviours would be to consistently respond to the needs that generate these behaviours.

So, how do we ensure that children are reassured that they can have their needs met on a reliable and consistent basis? Many of the strategies and approaches described in Chapter 3, though presented for their role in promoting secure attachment representations, are also of benefit in our endeavours to reassure children that their needs are acknowledged, understood and will be consistently met. In particular, I would refer the reader back to my earlier discussions regarding verbalizing understanding, responding to the need as well as the behaviour and enriching parental accessibility.

But is it enough to simply respond to the care requests of children on a consistent and predictable basis? Is this what an infant experiences in the context of sensitive, responsive and loving care?

Have you ever heard someone assert in an exasperated manner *you only ever do something for me if I ask*? It is my contention that infants are mostly cared for in a proactive manner. Because they do not have the capacity to physically approach us and communicate their needs and wishes to us in words, we stay close to them, anticipate their needs and respond to them.

Like infants, children are reassured about their accessibility to needs-provision when they experience adults as being aware of them and their needs and responsive to their needs without the child having to go to great lengths to make it so. Reactive caregiving, that is, caregiving that relies too much on children addressing their needs to adults before responding and too little on anticipating and responding to the child's needs before they do anything to call attention to their needs, conveys a message to children that they have to take matters into their own hands in order to obtain a caregiving response.

This kind of thinking can give rise to coercive and deceitful behaviours on the part of the children that has a negative impact on the promotion of secure dependency on adults in a caregiving role. In contrast, proactive caregiving reassures children regarding their accessibility to needs-provision. Emotional refuelling in reverse, as described in the previous chapter, is an excellent strategy for reassuring children that their parent is aware of them, thinking about them and their needs and prepared to respond to them. By reducing anxiety and associated preoccupations with accessing needs-provision, proactive caregiving is a powerful way of promoting children's exploration, opportunities for mastery experiences, and resilience.

The following is an aspect of caregiving that I think is essential to raising well-adjusted, resilient children. Research conducted by Harry Harlow[50] in the 1950s sought to identify what it is about caregiving behaviour that elicits an infant's love for its caregivers. In his research, Harlow identified the critical importance of *contact comfort* in reducing stress and eliciting loving behaviours in infants. Harlow separated infant rhesus monkeys from their mothers within 6 to 12 hours of birth and raised them with the aid of two forms of 'mother surrogate'. In one condition, the cage in which the infant rhesus monkey was accommodated contained a warm, soft 'mother surrogate'. This mother surrogate was shaped to feel like a mother, was wrapped in towelling to make it soft, was warmed by a light bulb placed behind it, and incorporated an artificial teat from which the infant nursed. The other mother surrogate was the same in every way, except that it was made of wire. What it lacked was softness.

Harlow found that the infant rhesus monkeys with the warm, soft mother surrogate sought and maintained contact with it, whereas the infants with the wire mother surrogate did not. In addition, the infants with the soft, warm mother surrogate thrived, whereas the infants with the wire mother surrogate also did not. In fact, monkeys that had the wire mother surrogate exhibited signs of psychological maladjustment and struggled to parent their own offspring. Furthermore, all infant rhesus monkeys displayed an apparent attachment to a heated gauze pad placed in the bottom of their cage and became distressed when this was removed, further emphasizing the importance of contact comfort in the development of attachment bonds over physical nourishment alone.

Harlow's research is consistent with what has been observed in populations of neglected and maltreated children, and also in the general population of children. My own research in the 1990s supported the idea that physical contact experiences are associated with psychological adjustment amongst teenagers.[51] Taken together, research shows that although physical nourishment is important, human beings will not thrive and become resilient unless they have access to warm and loving personal care that incorporates positive physical contact. The lesson of this research is that children benefit from contact comfort throughout their development, much as adults and adult relationships thrive in association with positive, safe and appropriate physical contact.

This is a challenging concept in a world where there is concern regarding the sad reality of sexual exploitation of children, the associated concern that children not be encouraged to engage in behaviour that might place them at risk, and the further concern that adults in a caregiving role not engage in behaviour that places them at risk of their intentions being questioned. My own personal experience has seen children in foster care denied contact comfort from caregivers who are worried about their intentions being misinterpreted and abuse allegations raised against them.

More generally, concern exists – certainly in my own country of Australia – for the development of boys in association with the lack of adult male role models in early learning environments. What is required is a sensible approach to this matter that is focused on the best interests of children. Children should be encouraged to seek, and should receive, contact comfort from their primary caregivers. Wherever possible, a child seeking contact comfort should be redirected to the nearest available primary caregiver. A child in distress who is seeking contact comfort from a known and responsible adult who has a clearly defined role in the child's life should also receive contact comfort, in the form of a hug, from such an adult where it is required and there is no primary caregiver present. The important point is that it is initiated by the child. Contact comfort should always be about the satisfaction of the child's need for regulation of their distress where a family member is not present. Contact comfort initiated by adults for the gratification of their own needs is not appropriate. Guidelines such as these regarding the provision of contact comfort can also encourage appropriate physical boundaries in overly affectionate children.

Finally, any discussion of children's needs would not be complete unless we mention how a society can ensure that children have reliable and consistent access to needs-provision. On a community level, children benefit from governments implementing social policies that safeguard their welfare and well-being, reduce poverty and support parents in their role as caregivers. A functional and effective child protection system that has responsibility for keeping children safe from harm but also recognizes the importance of preserving and strengthening existing attachment relationships is essential to ensuring that children are safe, loved and well-cared-for. An education system that provides children with a safe learning environment and access to educational and professional support in their learning endeavours is crucial to children realizing their intellectual potential.

Community supports for families, including equal access to medical and professional services, a social welfare system that guards against families experiencing overwhelming adversity, a public housing system that ensures all who need it have access to shelter, and a police force and judicial system that promotes safer communities are all essential to providing an environment in which children can access their needs and achieve their developmental potential, including their natural endowment to be resilient.

In summary, when a child is able to rely upon and predict consistent responses to their needs, and has a knowledge that this is the case, they are comforted and able to thrive and get on with exploring their world confidently and without anxiety. This is a vital component in the development of a child's resilience.

CHAPTER SUMMARY

- In order for children to achieve their developmental potential to be resilient and lead a full and satisfying life, they need to believe that they are able to satisfy their needs on a reliable basis.

- Important needs are often expressed as simple requests and wishes. Children need adults in a caregiving role to understand this.

- In the absence of reliable access to needs-provision, children experience anxiety.

- The anxiety that inevitably results from children not being able to consistently access a response to their needs, or the belief that this is the case, leaves children prone to emotional and behavioural difficulties. They often have a restricted range of interest that impairs their capacity to live a full and satisfying life.

- Children are reassured of their ability to access needs-provision in the context of parental care that is:
  - acknowledging and understanding
  - consistent in its responsiveness
  - proactive, as opposed to reactive.
- Children thrive in the context of care that is warm and loving and incorporates contact comfort.
- Community supports for families, including equitable access to medical and professional services, a social welfare system that guards against families experiencing overwhelming adversity, a public housing system that ensures all who need it have access to shelter, and a police force and judicial system that promotes safer communities are all essential to providing an environment in which children can access their needs and achieve their developmental potential, including their natural potential to be resilient.

A SHORT CONCLUSION

This book has described three key factors that assist children to achieve their birthright to be resilient – biological, psychological and environmental – as well as some ideas which I hope will prove helpful to caregivers in promoting resilience in children.

One thing I would like to stress in my final concluding comments is the importance of thinking not just about the child and their needs, but also yourself, the caregiver. Remember that, as a caregiver, you are in a position to profoundly influence a child's resilience.

Take care of your own physical and emotional health and try to achieve a good work–life balance. If you look after yourself, you are better equipped to be consistently involved with children in your care, to be understanding of their thoughts, feelings, wishes and intentions, to be responsive to these, and to be emotionally connected. This is very important, because the way in which you interact with children in your care influences how they think about themselves, how they feel, how they behave and how resilient they are when faced with challenges.

In his 1902 publication, *Human Nature and the Social Order*,[52] Charles Horton Cooley introduced the concept of the *Looking Glass Self* to portray his idea that how we see ourselves is based on our experiences relating to others.

Using naturalistic observation as his main research method, including observation of his own children, Cooley proposed that our ideas about ourselves incorporate:

1. our thoughts about how we must appear to others
2. our thoughts about the judgement of others of this appearance, and
3. our feelings associated with the imagined judgements of others – that is, we see ourselves in the way that we imagine others do.

Research has since shown that how adolescents and young adults think of themselves is related to how they think they are perceived by their parents.[53] It follows that a child's thoughts of how they must appear to others, how they think others judge them, and their associated feelings are likely to stem from a child's relationships with others.

Though not the sole factor, it is likely that if a child mostly experiences caregivers to be friendly and interested in them, understanding and accepting of who they are from an early age, the child will think of themself as interesting, competent and approved of. In contrast, if a child mostly experiences significant others to be inaccessible, rejecting or uninterested, they will think of themselves as bad, undeserving and unsafe.

I have in the past been asked by schools to conduct psychological assessments and provide direction for the care and management of their most challenging children. These are children who are difficult, disruptive, and time-consuming, who haven't responded to the schools' own responses, including disciplinary measures.

I interview and administer psychological questionnaires with the school, the children's parents and also interview the children in order to arrive at a diagnosis – commonly, the children will have an emotional disorder of some kind, such as an anxiety disorder or Reactive Attachment Disorder. I recommend psychological strategies to support the children and their behaviour, but a critical factor in the success of my work is that there is a change in the perception of teaching and support staff towards these children – from viewing them in negative terms to realizing that the behaviour stems from their emotional difficulties: from *bad* to *sad.*

The power of such a change in beliefs cannot be underestimated when one considers the impact of adult perceptions on the behaviour of children from the perspective of self-fulfilling prophecies. In Figures C.1 and C.2 you can see from two simple diagrams how a change of attitude on the part of the caregiver can have a transformative effect on the attitude and behaviour of the child.

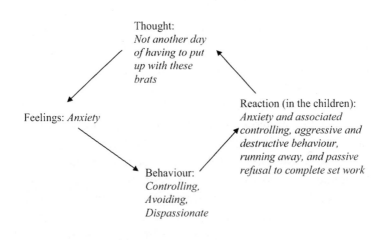

Figure C.1 *Negative self-fulfilling prophecies*

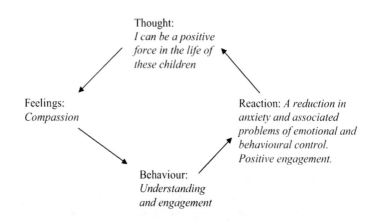

Figure C.2 Positive self-fulfilling prophecies

So, have positive expectations of the competency of children, their capacity to be resilient and take delight in their achievements! When children misbehave, as all children do, consider that there is always a reason for the behaviour and respond to the need as well as the behaviour. It is okay to be angry and frustrated with them from time to time, as children need to learn that relationships can be repaired.

I will finish with two allegories, the first drawn from the prologue of Paulo Coelho's acclaimed book *The Alchemist*,[54] in which he tells a story concerning the death of Narcissus, the boy who having knelt daily on the shores of a lake in order to contemplate his beauty in his reflection fell in and drowned.

Coelho tells that following the death of Narcissus the fresh water of the lake was transformed into salty tears, and that when asked by the goddesses of the forest why it wept, the lake replied that it wept for Narcissus.

Mistaking the meaning of the lake's response, the goddesses expressed understanding for its distress for only the lake had the opportunity to contemplate the beauty of Narcissus close at hand.

As Coelho tells the story, the lake replied that that it had not noticed that Narcissus was beautiful and that it wept because each time Narcissus had knelt before its shores it had been able to contemplate its own beauty reflected in the depths of Narcissus's eyes.

In another of his books, *The Zahir*,[55] Coelho tells the story of two firemen who, having been fighting a fire in the forest, take a break by a river. One's face is dirty and the other's face is clean. One washes his face and the other does not. The author poses the question as to which fireman washed his face. The answer is the fireman who already had a clean face, for he looked at the other and thought he was dirty.

Eyes are mirrors for a child's soul. What do children see in your eyes?

GLOSSARY OF TERMS

Aberrant: Behaviour that does not conform to societal standards and, as a result, damages relationships with others.

Accessibility: Having ready, easy, reliable and consistent access to basic human needs from an adult or adults who is/are in a caregiving role.

Activate: To make active, more active or capable of action.

Adaptation: Being able to successfully live in one's social environment.

Adaptive: Behaviour that enables an individual to live successfully.

Adversity: Hardship.

Affect: Emotion.

Affective attunement: Emotional connectedness, where two people express, and otherwise appear to experience, the same or similar emotion as each other.

Affect regulation: The capacity to control intensity of emotions for one's own benefit and in order to conform to conventional standards of emotional expression.

Anxiety: A pervasive feeling of worry or uneasiness, accompanied by physiological symptoms (e.g. sweating, palpitations, restlessness), and usually associated with an exaggerated perception of threat or danger.

Arousal: In this book, 'arousal' is used to refer to the level of activation of the nervous system.

Attachment: A term used to describe the dependency relationship a child develops towards his or her primary caregivers.

Attachment figure: Someone who provides physical and emotional care, has continuity and consistency in the child's life, and who has an emotional investment in the child's life.[56]

Attachment representations: The beliefs one has about self, others and the world.

Attunement experience: See **Affective attunement.**

Biological: To do with life or living things.

Birthright: Characteristics inherited from one's ancestors (though principally from one's parents) by right of birth.

Coercive: Behaviours that influence another party to behave in an involuntary manner (whether through action or inaction) by use of threats, intimidation, trickery, or some other form of pressure or force.

Cognitive-behavioural therapy: A treatment methodology that is based on theories of cognition and learning and the remediation of thoughts and behaviours that precipitate and maintain maladjustment.

Competence: Being capable of performing tasks of daily living.

Compulsion: A seemingly irresistible act performed in response to an impulse. In the context of this book, the impulse is to obtain reassurance regarding accessibility to needs-provision.

Conventional: Accepted customs or standards in a society or culture.

Debilitating: Causing a loss of energy or strength or vitality.

Dependency: Relying on others to sensitively, accurately and reliably respond to your needs and reasonable wishes.

Developmental deficit: Refers to a condition under which a child fails to achieve a normally expected developmental milestone.

Developmental delay: Refers to a condition whereby the development of an infant or child is slower than is normally expected.

Developmental milestone: Skills and abilities that most children learn at a certain age.

Developmental psychology: The scientific study of how children develop, including fine and gross motor development, language development, emotional development, social development, moral development and cognitive development.

Diagnosis: The process of categorizing behaviour through evaluation of a person's history, presentation, the person's own reports concerning their behaviour and the reports of others who know them.

Dissociation: A process by which a person becomes detached from their immediate environment. A defence that develops in response to intolerably high levels of stress.

Emotional refuelling: Restoring an infant or child's emotional well-being and confidence.

Empathy: The capacity to see things from the perspective of another person.

Empirical evidence: Refers to knowledge or information that is gathered through scientific study.

Endowment: Natural abilities or qualities. See also **Birthright**.

Environmental: To do with the external world.

Evolutionary: Used to refer to characteristics and behaviour that have been passed on from generation to generation as they serve a useful purpose in the survival of the species.

Exploitation: To take advantage of someone.

Genetic Inheritance: See **Endowment** and **Birthright**.

Hyperarousal: Arousal that is too high for effective action and optimal emotion and behaviour.

Infants: Children 0–2 years of age.

Innate: A natural or inherited characteristic or ability.

Insecure attachment: An outcome whereby an infant has either failed to learn that he or she can consistently depend upon their primary caregiver(s) to love, nurture and protect them, or has learnt that he or she cannot consistently depend upon their primary caregiver(s) to love, nurture and protect them.

Instinctive: Unthinking.

Interactive repair: An action on the part of a caregiver adult whereby they positively re-connect with a dependent child in association with having had to admonish the child or otherwise discipline them from engaging in inappropriate behaviour or affective displays.

Internalize: A process by which an idea becomes a semi-permanent aspect of a person's belief system.

Maladaptive: Beliefs, behaviours and affective displays that compromise the person's success in living on their environment.

Maltreatment: Physical, emotional and sexual abuse and neglect.

Mastery: To successfully achieve all requirements of a task or activity; usually associated with feelings of achievement and self-esteem.

Naturalistic observation: Involves observing the subject in its natural environment as unobtrusively as possible.

Obsessive: A preoccupation with something that impairs functioning.

Potent: Strong and capable.

Preoccupied: Distracted.

Primary attachment relationships: The attachment relationships the child has with his or her main caregivers.

Primary dependency relationships: The relationship(s) between the infants and the person or persons who are their primary caregivers.

Psychological: To do with the mind and mental life.

Psychology: The science of the mind or mental life.

Psychotherapy: The use of psychological theories and methods in the treatment of mental disorders.

Resilience: That quality of the individual that enables them to persist in the face of challenges and recover from difficulty or hardship. The application of adaptive coping skills under conditions of adversity, such that a child's circumstances and future capacity to cope with adversity are maintained or enhanced.

Secure attachment: An outcome whereby an infant has learnt the he or she can consistently depend upon their primary caregiver(s) to love, nurture and protect them.

Socialization: The process of learning about the culture of one's social world and how to live in accordance with it.

Stranger reaction: Usually observed in infants and young children, it is recognized in the child seeking closeness or otherwise orienting to their primary attachment figures in the presence of a person who is relatively unknown to them. The classic sign of the stranger reaction is when young children stand slightly behind and cling to their parent's leg while shyly gazing at a relatively unknown person.

Stressors: Anything that causes a person to experience stress.

Temperament: A person's typical mood, disposition or personality characteristics.

Trauma: An emotional or psychological injury, usually resulting from an extremely stressful or upsetting life experience.

ABOUT THE AUTHOR

Colby Pearce is the Principal Psychologist at Secure Start, a private psychology practice that specializes in providing services to children, adolescents and families in Adelaide, South Australia. A graduate of the University of Adelaide, he was first registered to practice as a psychologist in 1995. His work since registration has incorporated the provision of assessment and psychotherapy services in the areas of child protection, family law, inter-country adoption, refugees and community child and family psychology. He was the founder and Director of the Child Well-being Clinics, Master of Psychology training clinics that operated between 2006 and 2008 as a joint initiative between the University of South Australia and Families SA, and which provided a psychology service to maltreated children.

Colby has extensive experience in teaching and training of psychologists and other professionals and nine international publications in child and adolescent mental health, including his 2009 publication *A Short Introduction to Attachment and Attachment Disorder*. His 1994 publication *Predicting Suicide Attempts Among Adolescents* contributed to an Australia-wide general practitioner education and awareness program concerning adolescent suicidality. He is regularly called upon to speak about the care and management of maltreated children. He is married with three young children.

ENDNOTES

1. Nietzsche, F. in Frankl, V.E. (1985) *Man's Search for Meaning*. New York, NY: Pocket Books.

2. Nietzsche, F. (2003) *Thus Spoke Zarathustra*. Translated by R.J. Hollingdale. London: Penguin.

3. Nietzsche, F. in Frankl, V.E. (1985) *Man's Search for Meaning*. New York, NY: Pocket Books.

4. Frankl, V.E. (1959) *Man's Search for Meaning*. Boston, MA: Beacon Press.

5. Frankl, V.E. (1985) *Man's Search for Meaning*. New York, NY: Pocket Books, p.135.

6. Frankl, V.E. (1985) *Man's Search for Meaning*. New York, NY: Pocket Books, p.135.

7. Damasio, A.R., Grabowski, T.J., Bechara, A., Damasio, H., *et al.* (2000) 'Subcortical and cortical brain activity during the feeling of self-generated emotions.' *Nature Neuroscience 3*, 1049–1056

8. Based on Nietzsche, F. (2003) *Thus Spoke Zarathustra*. Translated by R.J. Hollingdale. London: Penguin.

9. Perry, B.D., Pollard, R.A., Blakley, T.L., Baker, W.L., and Vigilante, D. (1995) 'Childhood trauma, the neurobiology of adaptation, and 'use-dependent' development of the brain: How 'states' become 'traits'.' *Infant Mental Health Journal 16*, 4, 271–289.

10. Tomatis, A.A. (1991) *The Conscious Ear: My Life of Transformation through Listening*. New York, NY: Station Hill Press.

11. Rauscher, F., Shaw, G., and Ky, K. (1993) 'Music and spatial task performance.' *Nature 365*, 611.

12. Wilson, T., Brown, T. (1997) 'Reexamination of the effect of Mozart's music on spatial task performance.' *Journal of Psychology 131*, 4, 365.

13. Campbell, D. (1997) *The Mozart Effect: Tapping the Power of Music to Heal the Body, Strengthen the Mind, and Unlock the Creative Spirit.* New York, NY: William Morrow and Company.

14. Campbell, D. (2000) *The Mozart Effect for Children: Awakening Your Child's Mind, Health and Creativity with Music.* New York, NY: William Morrow and Company.

15. Bridgett, D.J. and Cuevas, J. (2000) 'Effects of listening to Mozart and Bach on the performance of a mathematical test.' *Perceptual and Motor Skills 90*, 1171–1175.

16. Thompson, W.F., Husain, G. and Schellenberg, E.G. (2001) 'Arousal, mood, and the Mozart effect.' *Psychological Science 12*, 3, 248–251.

17 Thompson, W.F., Husain, G. and Schellenberg, E.G. (2001) 'Arousal, mood, and the Mozart effect.' *Psychological Science 12*, 3, 248–251.

18. Van Der Kolk, B. (2006) 'Clinical implications of neuroscience research in PTSD.' *Annals of the New York Academy of Sciences 1–17.*

19. Van Der Kolk, B. (2006) 'Clinical implications of neuroscience research in PTSD.' *Annals of the New York Academy of Sciences 1–17.*

20. Damasio, A.R., Grabowski, T.J., Bechara, A., Damasio, H., *et al.* (2000) 'Subcortical and cortical brain activity during the feeling of self-generated emotions.' *Nature Neuroscience 3*, 1049–1056.

21. Van Der Kolk, B. (2006) 'Clinical implications of neuroscience research in PTSD.' *Annals of the New York Academy of Sciences 1–17.*

22. Pearce, C.M. (2010) 'An integration of theory, science and reflective clinical practice in the care and management of attachment-disordered children – A Triple A approach.' *Educational and Child Psychology (Special Issue on Attachment) 27*, 3, 73–86.

23. Tomatis, A.A. (1991) *The Conscious Ear: My Life of Transformation through Listening.* New York, NY: Station Hill Press.

24. Reite, M. and Field, T (1985) *The Psychobiology of Attachment and Separation.* Orlando, FL: Academic Press.

25. Crittenden, P.M. (1992) 'Quality of attachment in the preschool years.' *Development and Psychopathology 4*, 209–241.

26. Schore, A. (1994) *Affect Regulation and the Origin of Self: The Neurobiology of Emotional Development.* Hillsdale, NJ : Lawrence Erlbaum Associates.

27. Shakespeare, W. (1987) *Hamlet.* G.R. Hibbard (ed.) Oxford: Oxford University Press.

28. Ainsworth, M., Blehar, M., Waters, E. and Wall, S. (1978) *Patterns of Attachment: A Psychological Study of the Strange Situation.* Hillsdale, NJ: Lawrence Erlbaum Associates.

29. Bowlby, J. (1969) *Attachment and Loss, Volume I: Attachment.* New York, NY: Basic Books.

30. Bowlby, J. (1973) *Attachment and Loss, Volume II: Separation: Anger and Anxiety.* New York, NY: Basic Books.

31. Bowlby, J. (1969) *Attachment and Loss, Volume I: Attachment.* New York, NY: Basic Books.

32. Bowlby, J. (1969) *Attachment and Loss, Volume I: Attachment.* New York, NY: Basic Books.

33. Reite, M. and Field, T. (1985) *The Psychobiology of Attachment and Separation.* Orlando, FL: Academic Press.

34. Bowlby, J. (1973) *Attachment and Loss, Volume II: Separation: Anger and Anxiety.* New York, NY: Basic Books.

35. Bowlby, J. (1980) *Attachment and Loss, Volume III: Loss: Sadness and Depression.* New York, NY: Basic Books.

36. Main, M., Kaplan, N. and Cassidy, J. (1985) 'Security in Infancy, Childhood and Adulthood: A Move to Level of Representation.' In I. Bretherton and E. Waters (eds) 'Growing points of attachment theory and research.' *Monographs of the Society for Research in Child Development 50*, 66–104.

37. Ainsworth, M., Blehar, M., Waters, E. and Wall, S. (1978) *Patterns of Attachment: A Psychological Study of the Strange Situation.* Hillsdale, NJ: Lawrence Erlbaum Associates.

38. Egeland, B. and Farber, E.A. (1984) 'Infant-mother attachment: Factors related to its development and changes over time.' *Child Development 55*, 753–771.

39. Kinniburgh, K.J., Blaustein, M., Spinazzola, J. and Van Der Kolk, B.A. (2005) 'Attachment, self-regulation and competency: A comprehensive intervention framework for children with complex trauma.' *Psychiatric Annals 35*, 5, 424–430.

40. Prior, V. and Glaser, D. (2006) *Understanding Attachment and Attachment Disorders: Theory, Evidence and Practice.* London: Jessica Kingsley Publishers.

41. Howes, C. (1999) 'Attachment Relationships in the Context of Multiple Caregivers.' In J. Cassidy and P.R. Shaver (eds) *Handbook of Attachment: Theory, Research and Clinical Applications* (pp.671–687). New York, NY: The Guilford Press.

42. Pearce, C.M. (2010) 'An integration of theory, science and reflective clinical practice in the care and management of attachment-disordered children: A Triple A approach.' *Educational and Child Psychology (Special Issue on Attachment) 27*, 3, 73–86.

43. Cook, A., Spinazzola, J., Ford, J., Lanktree, C., *et al.* (2005) 'Complex trauma in children and adolescents.' *Psychiatric Annals 35*, 5, 390–398.

44. Damasio, A.R., Grabowski, T.J., Bechara, A., Damasio, H., *et al.* (2000) 'Subcortical and cortical brain activity during the feeling of self-generated emotions.' *Nature Neuroscience 3*, 1049–1056.

45. Van Der Kolk, B. (2006) 'Clinical implications of neuroscience research in PTSD.' *Annals of the New York Academy of Sciences 1–17*.

46. Pearce, C. (2009) *A Short Introduction to Attachment and Attachment Disorder.* London: Jessica Kingsley Publishers.

47. Pearce, C. (2009) *A Short Introduction to Attachment and Attachment Disorder.* London: Jessica Kingsley Publishers.

48. Reite, M. and Field, T (1985) *The Psychobiology of Attachment and Separation.* Orlando, FL: Academic Press.

49. Damasio, A.R., Grabowski, T.J., Bechara, A., Damasio, H., *et al.* (2000) 'Subcortical and cortical brain activity during the feeling of self-generated emotions.' *Nature Neuroscience 3*, 1049–1056.

50. Harlow, H.F. (1958) 'The Nature of Love.' *American Psychologist 13*, 673–685.

51. Pearce, C.M., Martin., G. and Wood, K. (1995) 'Significance of touch for perceptions of parenting and psychological adjustment among adolescents.' *Journal of the American Academy of Child and Adolescent Psychiatry 34*, 160–167.

52. Cooley, C.H. (1902) *Human Nature and the Social Order.* New York, NY: Scribner Publishers.

53. Cook, W.C. and Douglas, E.M. (1998) 'The looking glass self in family context: A social relations analysis.' *Journal of Family Psychology 12*, 3, 299–309.

54. Coelho, P. (1993) *The Alchemist.* London: Harper Collins.

55. Coelho, P. (2005) *The Zahir.* London: Harper Collins.

56. Howes, C. (1999) 'Attachment Relationships in the Context of Multiple Caregivers.' In J. Cassidy and P.R. Shaver (eds) *Handbook of attachment: Theory, research and clinical applications.* New York, NY: The Guilford Press.

INDEX

Lightning Source UK Ltd.
Milton Keynes UK
UKOW04f0642130414

229852UK00004B/20/P